Out of Their Faces and Into Their Shoes

OUT OF THEIR FACES

AND INTO

THEIR SHOES

How to Understand Spiritually Lost People and Give Them Directions to God

JOHN KRAMP

BROADMAN
& HOLMAN
PUBLISHERS

Nashville, Tennessee

© 1995
by John Kramp
All rights reserved
Printed in the United States of America

4261-83
0-8054-6183-3

Published by
Broadman & Holman Publishers
Nashville, Tennessee

Dewey Decimal Classification: 248.5
Subject Heading: Evangelistic Work \ Witnessing
Library of Congress Card Catalog Number: 94-38974

Unless otherwise noted, Scripture quotations are taken from the
Holy Bible, New International Version, © 1973, 1978, 1984, by
the International Bible Society.

Some names and situations used in this book have been changed to
protect the privacy of the people involved.

Library of Congress Cataloging-in-Publication Data
Kramp, John
    Out of their faces and into their shoes : how to understand spiritu-
ally lost people and give them directions to God / by John Kramp
       p.   cm.
    ISBN 0-8054-6183-3
    1. Witness bearing (Christianity). 2. Evangelistic work.   I. Title.
    BV4520.K66   1995
    248'.5—dc20
                                                                94-38974
                                                                CIP

To Lynn Marie:

toughest editor
greatest encourager
best friend
partner in life

Table of Contents

Part Four: Secrets of a Successful Search

The 24 Laws of Lostology / 185

Acknowledgments

Many people shared in the adventure of writing this book and deserve far more than words of gratitude.

To my parents, Bill and Hellen Kramp. They prove once and for all that Ward and June Cleaver of "Leave It to Beaver" fame were not a mythical couple. In fact, Ward and June were amateur parents compared with Bill and Hellen. In this writing project, as they have throughout my life, my parents have sacrificed without hesitation, encouraged me consistently, and loved me unconditionally.

To my daughters, Courtney and Kelly. They supported me during the long process of writing this book. (Plus they only fussed a little when I tied up the computer!)

To my co-laborers in Oregon, Steven Zink and Dwight Nall. They sacrificed personally and professionally to help begin a new church in a tough place that would reach spiritually lost people.

To Cecil Sims, David Palmer, Harold Hitt, and others from the Northwest Baptist Convention who gave their time, wisdom, and encouragement freely to our "baby church." They lived as lostologists long before I learned my first lessons and I value them as mentors.

To the people of Westside Baptist Church in Lake Oswego, Oregon. Many of them opened my eyes to lostology as they invited me into their lives as they struggled to find Jesus Christ. Later, they paid me the ultimate compliment by helping me get involved in the lives of their lost friends. No group of people could have given more, or done more, or worked harder to become a group of people who loved God and loved people with creativity, passion, and joy.

To my "go the second mile" friends and family members. They read through various editions of the manuscript and offered insights and guidance that strengthened this book beyond measure. So to Gene Mims, Chuck Kelly, Bill and Hellen Kramp, Ruth Kramp, Henry Webb, Jim Johnson, Mark Coppenger, David Francis, Roy and Anna Marie Edgemon, Mark Scott, Ron Keck, Steven Zink, and Jeff Iorg, I say a major thank you.

To my agents and friends, Mike Hyatt and Robert Wolgemuth. They believed in this project when it was only an idea and offered their expertise and guidance throughout each phase of the process. Without them, this book would have never been written. I believe they are the best at what they do and count it a privilege to be associated with them.

To Bill Hybels, Bill Bright, Robert Coleman, and Rick Warren. These men are some of my spiritual heroes. Their kind endorsements were some of the best surprises in this entire project.

To the folks at Broadman and Holman Publishers. They caught the vision for lostology and were willing to take a risk on a very unusual book about evangelism. So to Chuck Wilson, Bucky Rosenbaum, Forrest Jackson, Kirk Freeman, Greg Webster, and all the others on the B&H team, I say a heartfelt thank you.

"People that are nowhere are coming here
cause there's people they think are somewhere.
So everybody is really looking for some kind of answer
where there isn't one.
Why would 300,000 people come to anything
just because it's music.
Was music all that important?I don't think so.
People don't know.
They don't know how to live.
And they don't know what to do.
And they think if they can come,
they can find out what it is or how to maintain with it.
It's like people are really *lost*, I think."

young man on the way to
the Woodstock Festival August 1969 [1]

Introduction

Lostology
The study of being lost
and what that experience
can teach Christians about evangelism.

Christians and non-Christians agree on one thing—both dislike evangelism. The word alone conjurs up images of "in your face" confrontation. Therefore Christians usually avoid gospel showdowns and most non-Christians are relieved they do.

When evangelism is attempted it rarely begins with *"in your shoes"* empathy. If Christians really understood the spiritually lost people around them, they would talk about faith more naturally. Evangelism would be more of a conversation and less of a high-pressure sales pitch.

Unfortunately, most Christians do not understand non-Christians. We do not know what they think or how they feel, so we do not know how to help them. Even though we know what they need—a personal relationship with Jesus—we cannot get the conversation started. So we often say nothing.

Yet there is a simple way Christians can understand and help spiritually lost people. The secret is *lostology*, and that is what this book is about.

Jesus: The First, Great Lostologist

In describing His mission on earth, Jesus said, "For the Son of Man came to seek and to save what was lost" (Luke 19:10). Jesus knew anyone who can say "I'm lost" is a person to be envied.

When you say "I'm lost," you tell the world you have purpose. There is some place you need to be and you are not there. Without a destination, you can say "I lack direction," but you cannot say "I'm lost."

When you say "I'm lost," you tell the world you have value. Someone feels a sense of loss because you are not where you are supposed to be. If no one cares where you are, you can say "I'm alone," but you cannot say "I'm lost."

By using the word *lost*, Jesus helped us understand the nature of our relationship with God before we became Christians:

- By describing us as "lost," Jesus told us we have spiritual purpose. From God's perspective, there is a place we should be. God created us to be in a relationship with Him and if we are not with Him, we are spiritually lost.

- By describing us as "lost," Jesus told us we have spiritual value. We are not disposable. God cares that we are not where we should be and values us enough to search for us when we are spiritually lost.

God did for us what we could not do for ourselves: He declared us spiritually lost. Jesus built His ministry around this foundational understanding of our relationship with God.

When He taught about salvation and evangelism, Jesus told stories about three subjects: lost sheep, lost coins, and lost sons. Each of these parables in Luke 15 is profound in its simplicity:

- A shepherd had one hundred sheep. One got lost, so the shepherd left the ninety-nine in the fold to look for the one in the field. When he found the lost sheep, the shepherd celebrated.

- A woman had ten coins. One got lost, so she searched the house until she found the missing coin. When she found it, the woman celebrated.

- A father had two sons. One got lost, so the father waited expectantly for the boy to return home. When the lost son was found, the father celebrated.

In each story Jesus linked lostness with evangelism. He made a connection between being lost physically and being lost spiritually.

INSIDERS AND OUTSIDERS

As God in the flesh, Jesus was the ultimate spiritual insider, yet He related easily with lost people. During His earthly ministry, Jesus spent so much time with secular people that His critics accused Him of being "a friend of tax collectors and 'sinners'" (Matt. 11:19). Strange but true, when God came to earth, He lived among the lost and the lost loved Him.

Throughout His ministry, Jesus tried to build bridges between religious insiders and secular outsiders. He regularly debated religious leaders over the importance of reaching the spiritually sick and downcast. Jesus used analogies and told stories to help them sense His mission and understand His passion.

First Jesus compared Himself to a physician. "To whom does a physician go?" He asked the Pharisees, "to the sick or to the well?" (See Matt. 9:12). Not a Harvard entrance exam question, but the religious bunch missed it. Surely they understood His words. They just missed the point.

Jesus tried again. This time He used stories to explain His work—stories that went straight for their hearts. He dug for an emotional experience they all understood—being lost.

In His stories, Jesus communicated the foundational principles of lostology:

- Draw on what you already know from the physical experience of losing valuables and looking for them.

- Connect your experience to the way God feels about those who are spiritually lost.

- Use the insights you gain to shape your behavior and to guide your attitudes as you relate to people who are spiritually lost.

Jesus, the professor, enrolled the Pharisees in "Lostology 101." They flunked the course.

WE JUST DON'T GET IT

The Pharisees never got it. Trapped in their insider's perspective, they never connected with the world of lost people around them. So Jesus canceled the class and continued to live as a lostologist in their midst.

Our churches today are also filled with spiritual insiders who just do not get it. Stand in front of the Sunday morning church crowd and ask, "How many of you grew up in the church and have been part of the church most of your lives?" The majority of people will raise their hands. This is the problem. We, the Christian *insiders*, are called to reach the *outsiders*. But the *insiders* have been inside so long, we struggle to relate to the *outsiders*. Therefore we need to become lostologists . . . just like Jesus.

LOSTOLOGY: A NEW DISCIPLINE

Since lostology is a new field of study, it is appropriate to explain my credentials for writing in this discipline.

First, I made it up.

Second, I have been lost way more than your average person. When my internal gyroscope was installed, a few screws were left over. This has caused mild but chronic malfunctions in my directional system (like a hamster dropped by a preschooler once too often.)

Add to my daytime confusion the fact that I am a regular sleepwalker and my qualifications as a lostologist soar. Over the years, I have awakened in a quirky array of locations, unsure as to how I arrived, but fairly certain it was not good to be there.

Counting both day and nighttime lostness, I estimate I have averaged at least an hour a week being lost. By my calculation, I have logged approximately 1,976 hours of lostness—that's 82.33 days! Since lostology is still an emerging field of study, few benchmarks exist against which to measure personal statistics. For now, I must conclude that my record is above average and may even provide a standard for future scholars in lostology.

My third qualification for writing about lostology is my status as a cradle-roll-to-pastor church insider. Raised in a "Leave It to Beaver" home with godly parents, I cannot remember ever feeling uncomfortable in church. I went from Sunday School toddler to youth group teenager, on to college, then to seminary, and ultimately returned as a minister in the church that raised me. Church has always provided the backdrop for my life. The language, the subtle ways of doing things correctly, the biblical stories, the rituals—these are as much a part of my life as my breath. I have never known life apart from the church. In reality, I have been *in* so long I struggle to relate to those who are *out*. For the first ten years of my ministry, I had little contact with non-Christians: my life was the church. Little time was left for excursions into the world beyond the church walls.

My last and primary qualification for writing about lostology is that I started a church designed to reach secular people. Without that experi-

as a pastor, I have the same experience

I try to spend time w/ lost people by coaching my childrens sports teams.

ence, I never would have discovered the principles of lostology. For reasons I do not fully understand, God gave me the opportunity to begin a new church in Portland, Oregon—one of the most secular, least churched cities in America. That church, Westside Baptist, never grew large; the most we ever had was a couple of hundred people. But that meet-in-a-gymnasium, mobile church and the incredible people who became part of it taught me about lost people and lostology.

Those won to Christ introduced me to their friends. In time, their friends became my friends. Friendships deepened. Conversations became natural. For the first time, I had the chance to really talk with non-Christian people, to listen to them, to try to understand their perspectives on life. We talked about life, love, hope, and success. I shared my story. They shared theirs. These people marked my life. Like a missionary who steps into a foreign culture and can never fully return to his own, so I remain changed by what I experienced in those years.

In Portland, I understood for the first time how non-Christian people feel about embarking on a search for spiritual answers. I began to notice an emotional empathy with them. Their search reminded me of emotions I had experienced often, not as part of a spiritual quest, rather, as part of a physical experience—being lost. To my surprise, I discovered that my vast experience in being lost physically helped me identify with people who were lost spiritually.

Looking Backwards and Forwards

I left my church in Portland in April of 1992 to begin another ministry in Nashville, Tennessee. Since then, I have been reflecting on my experience—what my seeker friends taught me about being spiritually lost and what I have learned by getting physically lost myself. Jesus' stories about the lost and His search for the lost have also seasoned my thinking. New insights have come. I have become a lostologist. Now I am ready to share what I have learned with you.

Expectation's Check

Rather than focusing on *what* to say when you share your faith, lostology influences *how* you say *what* you say. Lostology helps you *How they* understand how lost people think and what lost people feel. This under- *think & feel* standing is especially important if you are a long-term spiritual insider and struggle to relate to spiritual outsiders. No matter what approach to evangelism you prefer—revival meetings, door-to-door visitation, a Sunday School outreach program, talking to strangers on airplanes, or a strategy of friendship evangelism—your training in lostology will help you be more effective in leading lost people to Christ.

PACE YOURSELF

The chapters in this book are relatively short. You could read them quickly and move on. I recommend another plan. Why not read two or three chapters a week; no more than a chapter a day? Give yourself time for reflection. Complete the questions at the end of each chapter. Meet with a group to discuss what you have learned and you will learn even more.

This book can help change the way you view life—the way you think about getting lost and the way you think about lost people. You are about to discover twenty-four ways to understand and help spiritually lost people . . . without being obnoxious. Before you know it, you will be a lostologist.

PART ONE

You Can Learn a Lot by Getting Lost

Lost . . . But Loving It

There is a way which seems right to a man,
but the end of that way is the way of death.
Proverbs 14:12

Lostology Law #1
Being lost can be fun.

Do you agree with the following description of secular people?

- Non-Christians are miserable.

- Felt-needs plague them.

- They struggle to build relationships.

- Nothing they do fills their empty lives with meaning.

- Aware of their sin, they run from God.

- They fear death and worry about eternity.

all of these are untrue.

What we believe about spiritual outsiders determines how we attempt to share the gospel with them. A few years ago, I would have affirmed the previous description. Such an inaccurate understanding accounted for, in part, my ineffectiveness in evangelism. Everything began to change when I learned the first law of lostology.

LITTLE CRATER LAKE

Like a twenty-six mile mirror, Crater Lake in southern Oregon rests in the stump of a once towering volcano. The brilliant blue of the water stuns first-time visitors. Encircled by multicolored lava walls up to two thousand feet high, Crater Lake demands to be remembered. That memory explains why a lone green sign changed our group's plans and sent us searching for *Little* Crater Lake.

Our original destination was Blue Lake, a beautiful little lake hidden in a maze of side roads and fir-treed hills east of Portland. One member of our group knew the way . . . well, sort of. Our caravan of minivans and cars sputtered up hills and around curves. Half the time, we were lost; the rest of the time, we were almost lost.

Along the way, we saw the sign: *Little* Crater Lake . . . 8 Miles. With visions of discovering a baby lake that would rival its mother's beauty, we agreed to check it out. Following a confusing course, we made our way to *Little* Crater Lake.

Our group pulled into a parking lot beside a large field of spindly grass; not a lake in sight. A wooden walkway stretched into the distance over a ridge. A small sign marked the walkway as the official entrance to *Little* Crater Lake. We loaded up children, chairs, and picnic equipment and began the walk, preparing for a not-to-be-forgotten view.

We topped the hill. There, nestled before us was *Little* Crater Lake: a twenty-foot, irregular circle of slimy, greenish-yellow water. Formed by a volcanic hiccup which exploded a narrow shaft of earth that later filled with water, the putrid pool sat stagnant and smelly. A lone sign warned, "No swimming."

Our group stood, stared, then collapsed in laughter. For us, *Little* Crater Lake instantly became a treasured memory, a testimony that being lost can be fun.

EVANGELICAL MISCALCULATION

For many years, I tried to share my faith in ways that violated some of the basic laws of lostology. Most of the evangelism methods I had learned were based on the premise that people believed in God, worried about eternity, and lived lives filled with felt-needs. These assumptions led me to accost people like a door-to-door vacuum salesman, regurgitating canned sales pitches without listening to or understanding their perspectives on life.

What a shock when I began to have close friends who were non-Christians. For the first time I encountered secular people with purposeful lives, strong families, a network of close friends, and multiple activities they enjoyed. What happened to the felt-needs, I wondered? To add to my predicament, many of these people lived with little concern for what would happen after they died. In a variety of ways, they created systems of theology or philosophy that insured they would fare well in whatever life was to come. My nice, canned pitches about God missed them completely. People without felt-needs did not fit well in my strategy of evangelism. It was definitely time for some lostology.

Basic Equipment

I began by asking, "Am I always miserable when I get lost?" My answer was no. Under certain circumstances, it is fun being lost, at least for a while. I recall times when, although I was lost, I stumbled onto delightful experiences that exceeded what I could have planned—like *Little* Crater Lake.

Jesus knew about the fun side of being lost. In Luke 15, He told a story about a man whose younger son left home loaded with his inheritance and a heart set on adventure. Armed with options, time, and money, the boy prepared to have fun.

Options? He had no place he needed to be, no specific destination in mind. He simply wanted adventure, so he headed for the distant county. His goal was to find a place where he could live as he wanted without his father's restrictions.

Time? Away from his father's house, time had become irrelevant. The prodigal had no one to answer to—he was free to do as he pleased. So he chased life to the edge and danced on the warning rail. As Jesus said, the boy spent his time in riotous living.

Money? Yes, he had more money than he ever dreamed possible. Bankroll in one hand, he grabbed life with the other. Friends and fun were his if money could buy them. He deprived himself no desire. When one day's party ended, he crawled into bed with a smile on his face.

Lost? Yes. But if you asked him, he would have said, "If this is lost, I'm loving it."

THE STRAIGHT STORY

The Bible pulls no punches. God never said sin is not fun or people cannot live enjoyable lives without God. At no point does Scripture attempt to discount the pleasures of sin. Instead, the Bible helps us understand that sin is always shortsighted. Focusing on today, sin forgets about tomorrow. That is why Solomon said, "a fool finds pleasure in evil conduct . . . " (Prov. 10:23), and the writer of Hebrews commended Moses for refusing to enjoy "the pleasures of sin for a short time" (Heb. 11:25).

FUN ON CREDIT

Do you receive credit card offers in the mail? Every week, financial institutions do all they can to insure that I use their cards to spend money I don't have. They offer bonuses, gifts, low interest rates, free airline tickets, and discount purchase packages to entice me into debt. Some send easy-to-use checks made out in blocks of five hundred to one thousand dollars so all I have to do to bury myself in debt is take those pieces of paper with me the next time I go shopping. Their sales hype focuses on how much I need things *now*. Missing is any reminder that if I do what they suggest, I will be enslaved to compound interest and will live as a financial sharecropper the rest of my life!

In the same way, sin offers *fun on credit*. We can charge today's pleasures on sin's credit card, but the bill will come. Sin may be fun, but it is never free. Ultimately, we will pay. Being lost can be fun, too, but only until the statement comes and the bills are due.

W. T. Purkiser said it well: "Sin would have few takers if its consequences occurred immediately."[1] Unfortunately, that is not the nature of sin.

LIVING WITHOUT FELT-NEEDS

On a Chamber of Commerce committee, I worked with a surgeon named Raji. He oozed money and power. Handsome features and a melodic accent added to the picture of a man who had achieved America's good life. At the time, he was building a million dollar home where he and his girl friend would live. People admired him and sought his guidance for medical concerns and community involvement.

I tried to talk with Raji about spiritual things. As we worked on the committee, I watched for openings to shift the discussion. We talked about his family and his life in India. He even shared his thoughts about the impact of religion on life in his county. I probed for any indication of dissatisfaction or needs in his life. Nothing surfaced. In time, he changed the direction of the conversation. Was he lost? Yes, no question. Was he miserable? Not in ways that showed. If receptivity to the gospel begins with felt-needs, Raji had few needs for starters. For the moment, he appeared to be lost . . . but loving it.

START WHERE PEOPLE ARE

When Christians assume all secular people are miserable, they miscalculate reality. The truth is, many have strong families, enjoy good relationships with networks of friends, and are involved in projects that give them a sense of meaning in their lives. Of course, this is not true in all cases, and it is not true forever. But to begin conversations with non-Christians assuming they have a strong awareness of their need for God is naive.

Ken Hemphill, president of Southwestern Baptist Theological Seminary, uses three questions to get spiritual conversations started with people he meets:

- What is your religious heritage?

- Has your heritage helped you answer the important questions you are asking in life?

- What are the questions you are asking?[2]

[margin note: 3 questions]

Dr. Hemphill's questions are great tools for lostologists. Asking these questions helps probe a lost person's receptivity-level before your plunge into a full explanation of the gospel. If the person shows no interest in the questions you ask, you may be talking to someone in the lost-but-loving-it stage. If this is the case, give a brief statement about the difference Jesus has made in your life and trust God to use the spiritual seed you plant.

[margin note: Good suggestion]

Christianity offers a Savior. Those with no sense of need easily reject the offer. Give it time. Along the way, resources run thin. Life presents challenges that sap all reserves. Needs, repressed or ignored, surface. At that point, the message of Christ starts to sound like good news.

Lostologists understand the seasons in people's lives. They know the futility of offering the answer to people who are not asking the question. They also know time will provide the opportunity. People can have fun being lost . . . but only for a while. Needs will surface; opportunities for sharing faith will come. When that happens, Christians must be there to point the way home.

THE LOSTOLOGY LAB

Are you ready for some lab work? Think of it like your biology class in high school. Do you remember? You read about grasshoppers, heard lectures about grasshoppers, watched films on grasshoppers, and memorized trivial tidbits of information about grasshoppers. Then one day you headed to the lab. Once there, your knowledge of grasshoppers changed forever. From a jar of formaldehyde, your teacher plopped a pickled grasshopper in front of you and told you to do an autopsy on it. That is when you learned an important distinction: it is one thing to read about grasshopper parts; it is another thing to slice one of those crunchy bugs into pieces with your own hands. Learning expands rapidly when you get personally involved with the subject matter . . . grasshoppers included!

Reading the chapters in this book will help you understand the concepts and basic content of lostology. But answering the questions in the Lostology Lab section at the end of each chapter will help you get involved. You will reflect on your personal experiences in being lost and recall your encounters with spiritually lost people. Do not forget what you learn. Record your insights so you can keep track of your lostological discoveries.

Cutting up grasshoppers with a group in lab class was always more fun than doing it alone. Same thing here. If it is possible to meet with a group of friends and study this material together, your learning experience will be greatly enriched. Perhaps you could meet once a week to discuss a few chapters and share your ideas and stories. Your insights as a lostologist will increase as you hear stories about times your friends got lost. Remember, lostology draws on all experiences of being lost, not just your personal experiences. That is why meeting in a group can be so valuable. With others, your learning experience multiplies.

Here are some lab questions to help get started:

- At this point in your study, how would you explain lostology to someone who asked about what you are reading?

- Recall a time when you got lost but ended up having a good time anyway. What happened? Who were you with? What made the experience pleasurable and memorable?

- Would you feel comfortable using the three questions Dr. Hemphill uses to get a spiritual conversation started? Why or why not? Have you ever used questions like these to get a conversation started? What questions did you use? What happened?

- Have you ever tried to share your faith with a non-Christian who was still in the lost-but-loving-it stage? How did he or she respond? What did you do? How did you feel?

- Have you known someone who was initially closed to the gospel but later, as circumstances in his or her life changed, became open to spiritual things? What brought the change? How long did it take?

- How do you feel right now about what you are learning about lostology? Do you think lostology will affect the way you do evangelism? How?

Coming Next: Living with Their Choices

People make choices that influence how their lives unfold. Some choices get you lost. As Christians, how should we respond when we meet these people? What should we assume about their lives and the choices they have made? Sure, they are lost. But did they get lost on purpose? We will find the answer in the second law of lostology.

Lost on Purpose?

Some people . . . have wandered from
the faith and pierced themselves with many griefs.
1 Timothy 6:10

Lostology Law #2
No one gets lost on purpose.

A mother stands in the narrow aisle of a crowded department store. She feels it before she knows it: her little boy, Bobby, is missing. Two contradictory emotions kick into gear simultaneously—fear and anger.

Enter emotion number one. Fear floods her mind with frightening possibilities. She begins a frantic search, calling her child's name as she looks down each aisle. As she runs, she prays, "Oh God, keep Bobby safe."

Enter emotion number two. Anger replays high-speed highlights in her mind of the times Bobby was lost in the past. She continues to run, to call, and to search. She even continues to pray. Only now there is an undercurrent to the prayer, embarrassing but true: "Yes, God. Let Bobby be all right. Because when I find him, *I'm* going to kill him."

After some eternity-length minutes, the mother spots Bobby, standing by a rack of toys, oblivious to what he has just done to her. She grabs him by the shoulders and says, "Bobby, don't get lost like that again."

Bobby stares at her, a bewildered look on his face. Defensively, he says, "Gee Mom, I didn't get lost on purpose." He's right; he didn't. But he was lost all the same.

A LOST CHECKUP

The first step in the study of lostology is to reflect on some of the times you were lost. Your personal experiences become your lostology laboratory. To get started, we will take a guided memory-jog. Put on your mental tennis shoes and run through a rapid review of your lost highlights. Recall and describe specific times when you were lost:

- as a child in a store

- as you tried to follow directions

- in a large office building

- as you tried to find a room in a large hospital

- as you drove through a large city

Now that some of your lost experiences are vivid in your thinking, consider this question: Did you ever get lost on purpose? No. Although many of us get lost frequently, we always have reasons for getting lost. Those reasons never include getting lost on purpose.

UNDERSTANDING THE LOST

Jesus interacted constantly with spiritually lost people. To every relationship, He brought incredible insight into human nature coupled with complete understanding of theology. As God incarnate, Jesus knew everything about sin and sinners. The Bible reveals two foundational truths:

- Jesus knew the people He encountered were sinners by nature: "Surely I have been a sinner from birth, sinful from the time my mother conceived me." (David writing in Psalm 51:5.)

- Jesus knew the people he encountered were sinners by choice: "This is the verdict: Light has come into the world, but men loved darkness instead of light because their deeds were evil" (John 3:19).

In spite of their spiritual condition, Jesus did not "write off" people as lost on purpose. He, better than all others, knew the degree to which people could get lost. Jesus understood the consequences people endured as a result of their sin—consequences deserved but never desired. He dealt with sinners as if being lost was only a current location, not an unchangeable destination. Jesus lived with the awareness that the worst of sinners could become children of God.

Jesus tried to communicate His passion for the lost to the Pharisees—the religious elite of His day. They proved to be thick-headed and tough-hearted, so Jesus shifted gears and told them the three stories about lost sheep, lost coins, and lost sons. Even though the Pharisees missed the point, we can learn much from these stories. Therefore we will refer to them throughout our study of lostology.

What do these parables tell us about getting lost . . . from the perspective of the one who is lost:

- The lost sheep? Lost through *preoccupation*. He nibbled himself away from the flock and got lost. He was not paying attention to the right things.

- The lost coin? Lost through the *carelessness* of others. A victim, but lost all the same.

- The lost son? Lost through *miscalculation*. He knew what he wanted, where he could get it, and what it would cost. From his perspective, everything in his life added up to success. Small problem: he added wrong and ended up lost.

Contemporary spiritual applications for these three parables are easy to find:

- Have you known people who got lost spiritually due to preoccupation? Too much focus on a job? Money? Relationships?

- Have you met spiritual victims—people who grew up in secular homes without the opportunity to attend church or hear the gospel? Is it any wonder they got lost? Sure, they were responsible for being lost. But the circumstances in their lives did nothing to make things easier for them.

- Have you known people who miscalculated the true resources needed to live life and ended up spiritually bankrupt? They believed the lie and tried to live without their heavenly Father's influence and resources.

[handwritten margin note: VAGUE]

In each case, from the lost person's perspective, there were reasons for being lost: preoccupation, carelessness, miscalculation, and lots of others. But none got lost on purpose.

PARADE OF LOST SOULS

They were sitting on the couch outside the church office when I met them. Marie was young, fourteen years old, maybe fifteen. She claimed she was eighteen. Her dark hair, golden skin, and striking features should have combined to make her a beautiful young woman. But her dark eyes, dull and vacant, blurred the image. She stared at her hands as they fidgeted nervously in her lap. She did not speak, never looked up, never made eye-contact.

Andy sat beside her. He had curly, dirty-dishwater blond hair, a see-through mustache, and do-it-yourself tattoos on his forearms. Around twenty years old, he had a slight build but looked hard and muscular. They were married, he assured me. (I knew better.) All they needed was a little help, a job or some money. Andy was a talker—a salesman—one used to talking his way into help or out of trouble.

Neither of them knew it, but I was a hard man to deal with. One regular feature of life on the pastoral staff of a large, downtown church in Texas was the steady stream of people passing through asking for financial help. Over the years, these heart-wrenching requests for help had calloused me. Early on, I believed the stories. I handed out money, even arranged job interviews and provided lodging for the night in area hotels. But over and over, people burned me. In time, I struggled to believe anyone who stopped in with a hand out.

Still, like a parade of lost souls they came. Different faces with different stories. Sure they were lost. Yes, they were needy; they needed God's love more than anything else. Yet, it was easier to tell myself they were just getting the consequences of the choices they had made. This simplistic assessment made it easier for me to walk away with limited involvement and little emotional investment.

In the end, Andy and Marie took the limited help our church offered and ran, without thanks. Marie called me two weeks later. Andy was in jail; she wanted me to give her bail money. The same old story continued.

Perhaps it was all they could do given their situation. I now realize they did not set out to be where they were. Yes, they were lost. Carelessness? Possibly. Victims? Perhaps. Miscalculation? Unquestionably. Whatever the reason, they did not wreck their lives on purpose. No one does.

Starting Point

When we meet people who are lost spiritually, we should assume they never intended to damage their lives. Since they did not get lost on purpose, it is logical to assume they will be open to a new set of directions. This starting point helps us relate to secular people with positive expectations and love.

Jesus' stories of the lost sheep, the lost coin, and the lost son will help you probe the background of non-Christians you meet:

- Check for indications of spiritual carelessness—like the lost sheep. If people tell you they do not go to church, ask them why. Often you will discover they did not decide to quit going to church, they simply started doing other things. People who have been spiritually careless are often open to making a change in their lives. They simply need motivation and some positive directions.

- Check to see if you are dealing with spiritual victims—like the lost coin. Ask about their parents and the spiritual values they had. Often you will discover they were not encouraged to develop their spiritual lives. Their parents and family members may still be antagonistic to spiritual things. Be sensitive with these people. They are dealing with confusing emotions and loyalties. Be careful not to condemn their parents as irresponsible or unloving; such comments will prompt people to be defensive. Remain positive. Focus on the opportunity they now have to learn about spiritual matters and make their own informed decisions.

- Check to see if you are dealing with someone who is lost through spiritual miscalculation—like the lost son. Most people are sincere in their beliefs and have done all they can to make life work for them. They have simply miscalculated. Your interaction with them must be handled with sensitivity. Before they can make progress, they must admit they have been wrong. That is a tough admission for most of us to make. If you push too hard, many people will recoil and run. Take your time and watch for the awareness of miscalculation to dawn.

I have discovered that the more I learn about people's lives, the more willing I am to get involved with them spiritually. People make tragic mistakes. Sin blinds them until they hurt themselves and others in a spiral of destruction. Even when people celebrate their sin and flaunt their spiritual rebellion, the fact remains: no one plans to end up in a pig pen. It happens, but that doesn't mean it happens on purpose.

The Lostology Lab

Chapter 2 deals with how our expectations and beliefs about lost people influence our interaction with them. Consider these questions and probe your own expectations and beliefs:

- When you meet people who are spiritually lost, do you expect them to be open to hearing about Jesus Christ? Why or why not?

- In what ways do your expectations influence the way you raise spiritual issues with lost people?

- How would your approach change if you agreed that no one is lost on purpose so everyone should be open to a change of direction?

Think about some of the lost people you have met over the years:

- Have you known anyone who was lost through spiritual carelessness? Describe this person. Why did she neglect her spiritual life? Was she antagonistic to spiritual matters or simply too involved in other things? What happened when you tried to talk to her about your faith or your church?

- Have you known anyone who was a spiritual victim? Describe this person. What role did his family play in his attitudes toward Christianity? Was he critical of his background and the way his parents raised him? How did he respond when you attempted to talk with him about his relationship with Christ or about attending church?

- Have you known anyone who was lost through spiritual miscalculation? What did she believe about her spiritual life and the importance of a personal relationship with Christ? What did she believe happens to people after they die? What did she expect to happen to her? How did she respond when you talked with her about your faith?

COMING NEXT: A BOTTOM-LINE QUESTION

If people do not get lost on purpose, why *do* they get lost? Lostologists have pondered this question. The answer lies in the third law of lostology—the topic of our next study.

Why We Get Lost

For wide is the gate and broad is the road that
leads to destruction, and many enter through it.
Matthew 7:13

Lostology Law #3
It is easy to get lost.

As soon as the doctor smacked him on the bottom in the delivery room, Matt looked up and asked, "Why'd you do that?"

All right, so it didn't really happen . . . but it could have. My friend Matt is a question-asking machine. The months before he could talk were just a warm-up, a time to build up inventory. No other explanation accounts for the torrent of questions that flows from his mouth. Like a dam crumbled by a raging river, Matt's lips buckle against the flash flood of questions his brain creates. His red hair, freckled face, and impish smile provide the spillway for the thundering flow of questions that gush constantly through his lips.

When Matt was five, he spent the weekend at our house while his parents were away. If a count had begun on Friday night and ended on Sunday afternoon, Matt's questions would have easily hit four digits. I am not talking about easy-to-answer questions. Oh no, Matt specialized in the unanswerable:

- What if a space ship lands on the hood of the car while we're driving?

- What if Superman is driving that eighteen wheeler over there?

- What if pirates attack our car?

- What if a tree falls on the house while we're gone?

On Saturday afternoon, while waiting for a movie to start, I tried to distract Matt temporarily. Catching him mid-breath, I said, "Matt, how did you get to be so smart?" Without missing a beat, he gave me a self-assured look and said, "I ask a lot of questions."

AN ANSWER AT LAST

Pretty insightful for a five-year old. I should have asked Matt why people get lost. I have thought about that question. In fact, I have found the answer that has eluded philosophers, theologians, lostologists, and possibly even Matt. Why do we get lost?

We get lost because it is easy.

Pretty deep stuff, right? Don't miss the implication. If we get lost because it is easy, then getting lost belongs in a comprehensive category of life I have entitled:

Bad Things That Happen To You Automatically Unless You Take Specific Steps To Prevent Them from Happening

It is hard to get that title on a file folder but that's it. Here are some representative samples of things that fit in this life-category:

- getting fat

- hitting your thumb with a hammer

- stubbing your big toe

- getting sunburned

- cutting yourself shaving

- killing your house plants

- getting cavities

- getting knots in your shoe laces

- getting weeds in your yard

- getting stains on your new tie or dress

- sticking hot pizza to the roof of your mouth

Why do you get physically lost? Dig deep. Think hard. Consult the experts. Invest in years of psychotherapy. The ultimate answer is profound in its simplicity. You, like all of us, get lost because it is easy. You have to work to *avoid* getting lost. Do nothing special and you will get lost every time. Lost happens. Lost is life's default mode.

Speaking to a group of senior adults, Art Linkletter said, "Getting old is an amazing experience. You just live your life and then one day you're old. And you're really not sure how it happened."

What is true about aging is true about being lost spiritually. From a spiritual perspective, getting lost is unavoidable. Human nature is fundamentally flawed by sin. If people live their lives apart from God and follow their intuitions, they stay lost. That is because getting lost—physically or spiritually—is easy.

COMPELLING COMPASSION

Jesus understood how easily people become spiritually lost. He searched as the Good Shepherd for lost people. He went as the Great Physician to those who were spiritually sick.

It happened once at a private dinner party. (See Luke 7). A Pharisee named Simon invited Jesus to join him and his friends for the evening. They were reclining around the table when *she* walked in. Everyone knew her . . . at least knew about her. She had quite a reputation. No one in town qualified more completely for the title "sinner" than this woman. The group watched as she kneeled at Jesus' feet and began to cry. She kissed His feet and wet them with her tears. With her hair she wiped dust and dirt from His feet.

The Pharisees were indignant. Imagine a sinner like her walking in uninvited and beginning to wash a teacher's feet. Quickly, they condemned her to perpetual sinner status with no hope of parole. How little compassion they showed. To them, she was a wicked woman who chose a wicked life of sin and deserved sin's consequences.

Jesus responded to her differently. He refused to condemn her although He knew all about her sinful life. He did not allow Simon and the others to pronounce their slicing judgments in her presence as if she were not really there. To the surprise of His pious-puffed religious friends, Jesus addressed the woman directly. With gentleness, He honored her, her faith, and her love. Indeed, she had sinned. But Jesus offered His grace. To one who was lost, He offered hope that she could be found.

UNINTENTIONALLY LOST

Tom was lost when I met him. A successful salesman, raised in an affluent family, he had everything going for him. As we became friends and I learned his story, it was easy to see that many influences had converged to confuse him spiritually:

- decisions made by his parents about lifestyle and church involvement

- his friends and associates and the influence they had on his life

- career decisions that set the course for his life

- financial considerations that impacted his decisions

- his personal morality which caused him to rank well compared to others

All these factors and more led Tom to the place he was when we met. Why was he lost? Tom was lost for lots of reasons. Most of all, Tom was lost because lost is what happens unless you take specific actions to insure you do not get lost. His life provided striking evidence of the truth of Lostology Law #3: getting lost is easy.

NO BIG SURPRISE

As we encounter secular people, this thought should shape our thinking: these people are lost because it is easy to be lost. Over time, they simply lived their lives and moved further away from God. If we remember this, we will not be surprised by what lost people believe, say, and do:

- When talking to lost people, we must not react to what they believe. Do not say: "That's the stupidest thing I've ever heard." Or, "Don't tell me you believe that. My first grader knows more about the Bible than that!"

- In conversations, we must not be put off by things lost people say. Secular people often use language that offends us. How easy it is to react. Unfortunately, if we focus on people's vocabularies, we may miss the opportunity to tell them about Jesus— the only one who can ultimately change their hearts and thereby clean up their speech. Do not expect lost people to act differently from what they are—lost.

- Sometimes lost people test us by talking about things they have done in the past. They may be toying with us, seeing if they can prompt a reaction. More likely, they are checking the scope of our love and acceptance. Many lost people feel God cannot love them because of all the things they have done. If we wince at the mention of their sin and distance ourselves from them, they may assume God will do the same thing.

When we remember how easy it is to be lost, we guard against judging secular people harshly. Without God's grace and intervention in our lives, we could have done the same things as any of the lost people we meet. None of us are immune. Recalling God's intervention in our lives helps us respond with grace to lost people entrapped by sin.

An awareness of the basic principles of lostology prepares us to be patient with lost people. When they are ready for new directions, we will be there with empathy and love.

The Lostology Lab

Many longtime spiritual insiders forget how easy it is to be lost spiritually. Therefore, they tend to be shocked and judgmental when they interact with non-Christians. By reminding us that it is easy to be lost, this chapter helps us adjust our attitudes toward lost people. Check your attitude by answering the following questions:

- How do you view people who are spiritually lost?

- Have you considered how easy it is to be lost spiritually? If you recognize that it is easy to be lost, how does this impact the way you deal with lost people?

- How do you respond when non-Christians begin to tell you what they believe?

- What do you do if they use language that offends you?

- How do you respond when non-Christians begin to tell you about the wrong things they have done in their lives? Are you shocked? Are you judgmental? What do you say? What do you do?

- When you hear secular people describe the sin in their lives, do you think of them as morally inferior to you? If so, why? If not, why?

- As a lostologist who understands how easy it is to get lost, how will you attempt to deal with secular people in the future as you engage them in spiritual discussions?

COMING NEXT: SLIPPING INTO ANOTHER DIMENSION

There is something strange about being lost. When you are lost, it is as if you slip into another dimension of experience. You are never quite sure when and how you got there. All you know is that something has changed. Lostologists study this uncharted dimension. You have been there in the past. You will be there again. There is no way to escape. We will pay a visit in the next chapter.

The Lost Zone

Not everyone who says to me, "Lord, Lord,"
will enter the kingdom of heaven, but only he
who does the will of my Father who is in heaven.
Matthew 7:21

Lostology Law #4
You can be lost and not know it.

If you were watching television on Friday night in October 1959, you joined 18 million other viewers for the first episode of a new television show. You were greeted by discordant, haunting music and a voice that said:

You're traveling through another dimension.

A dimension not only of sight and sound but of mind.

A journey to a wondrous land whose boundaries are that of imagination.

A journey that will end in the Twilight Zone.

From 1959 until 1964, the raspy, rich voice of Rod Serling invited viewers to join him on that journey to the Twilight Zone. In each episode, a small caste of characters found themselves lost in a world gone awry. They entered the Twilight Zone but did not know it.

One show began with a man walking down a crowded downtown street. As he passed a woman collecting for charity, he pitched a coin into the cigar box on the table in front of her. Rather than falling flat, either heads or tails, this coin stood on its edge. That small action altered the world for the man who tossed it. Initially, he was unaware anything had happened. But from the moment the coin landed on edge until the coin fell, that man traveled in the Twilight Zone.

There is another zone unsuspecting travelers pass into unaware. Call it the *Lost Zone*. Like the man and his coin, these travelers enter the Lost Zone through a simple act, a minor miscalculation, a moment of distraction. Perhaps they miss a turn, veer right instead of left. Either way, they set a course that alters reality for them. From that moment on, aware or not, they live with new realities in the Lost Zone.

The Doorway In

Getting lost is a strange sensation. At a critical point, we make a decision then turn and head on our way. If the turn is wrong, we are technically lost. It makes no difference whether we feel lost or acknowledge that we are lost. Reality stands altered from that moment. We may drive for hours in the wrong direction, convinced that we are on course. But all the while, we are lost. The longer we continue in the wrong direction, the more lost we become.

A Lost Son in the Lost Zone

We could call Jesus' story about the wayward son, "The Lost Son in the Lost Zone." It clearly illustrates the Lost Zone principle.

The son made a decision to leave home with his share of the family inheritance. The moment he walked out the door, he made his wrong turn. From that point on, he was lost and became progressively more lost.

If anyone had asked him, he would have heartily denied that he was lost. On the contrary, he was convinced a life of grand freedom and adventure was beginning. And there was freedom. Undoubtedly, he did have adventure along the way. Life can be interesting in the Lost Zone.

Just like a classic "Twilight Zone" episode, life in the Lost Zone began to unravel for the prodigal son. Days of reckless living gave way to days of famine. Then famine reshaped his course in life until he ended up in a pig pen—an unthinkable situation for one raised in affluence. But he was in his new reality, a reality that began when his father's door slammed and the boy took his first step into the Lost Zone.

Lost at Lunch

I always assumed people who were spiritually lost accepted the fact they were lost. Wrong. Many don't.

One day I had lunch with a businessman named Brian. I had heard about him for months through one of his friends who attended our church. Brian had been adamant about his lack of interest in church or Christianity. In fact, when asked about spiritual things, Brian had responded to his friend, "I'll believe in Jesus Christ the day he comes walking through that door." To me that was a pretty good indication that Brian was lost and knew it.

Through a fascinating series of divinely orchestrated events, Brian and his wife attended a service at our church. He was warm and responsive to me so I suggested we get together for lunch and get acquainted. I did not know what to expect from the meeting. As usual, I planned to be low-key and talk about spiritual matters to the degree of Brian's interest or openness.

After informal chitchat, our meal came. When meeting with secular people, I always feel a bit uneasy at the beginning of a meal. My normal practice is to say a prayer of thanks for my food, even in a public place. Not to do so feels hypocritical. Yet, doing so can make my new friends uncomfortable. So I try to be sensitive to each situation.

That was my struggle with Brian as the waitress brought our food. When she left, Brian shocked me when he said, "I'd like to say a prayer if you don't mind." Trying to hide my surprise, I said, "Sure, that would be great." We bowed our heads and Brian recited from memory a prayer used by his college fraternity. It was the kind of prayer you would expect out of a fraternity handbook. Still, I was amazed he remembered it and wanted to pray it.

Had I read him wrong? Was he really a Christian? The more we talked that day and in the days that followed, the more I knew Brian was lost indeed. But he was lost and didn't know it. He was caught in that altered state of reality called the Lost Zone.

Searching in the Lost Zone

Many secular people are just like Brian. Their sense of spiritual reality is skewed. At some point in the past, they took a wrong turn spiritually. They may have been unaware there was a turn to miss. Nor do they have any idea how far they have gone in the wrong direction.

An "in your face" attempt to force secular persons to admit they are lost, usually builds resistance rather than receptivity. Launching into a gospel presentation assuming they know they are lost and are ready for a new direction can be counterproductive.

POSITIVE STEPS

We must discern how people view the spiritual dimension of their lives. The best way to do this is to ask questions. I have found two questions surface the issues with many people:

good questions

- What do you think happens to people after they die?

- Why do you believe that?

Many secular people believe in God and some sort of life-after-death. They believe that people end up in some sort of positive place after they die, because they did the best they could while they lived and because God is a God of love. Others view heaven as the final terminal to which all tracks lead. They expect God to accept all who followed their path as best they could. Others throw in more variations of life-after-death alternatives. By asking how people view eternity, you can get a clue into how they perceive their spiritual status.

The second question probes the basis for their beliefs and reveals more insights. Non-Christians tend to rely on their own interpretations of theology as the foundation for their beliefs. Few know what the Bible says so they make no reference to it. In fact, they assume all ideas about God are pretty much equal so their ideas have as much validity as those held by anyone else. It is not unusual to talk with secular people who argue passionately about their views of life-after-death and who base their views on their personal perspectives alone.

With the proliferation of Christian teachings on radio and television, it is common to talk with people who can answer the question about eternity correctly and affirm that they are Christians and will go to heaven when they die. Be careful. Ask them to explain why they believe they will go to heaven. Many will point to the good lives they have lived. They will not mention Jesus' death or their sins. Simply put, they miss the plan of salvation all together. They are lost and do not know it.

A New Map

Our responsibility is to give non-Christians a new spiritual map, the map of the gospel, and help them see life from a new perspective. We start with the truth in Christ and show how Jesus is The Way. All of us have taken a wrong turn and ended up in the Lost Zone. All of us need to take the U-turn of repentance and travel in the direction God has for us.

For most people, especially secular adults, this process takes time. Part of God's convicting work in people's lives is creating an awareness that something is wrong. In ways they cannot fully articulate, they begin to sense they may be lost. Once that uneasiness settles around them, they become open to looking for a new map to direct their lives.

The Lostology Lab

Can you think of a time when you were lost physically but did not know it? Focusing on that experience, how it happened and how you felt, can help you empathize with non-Christians who are spiritually lost and are unaware. See if these questions help you reflect on your experience:

- What factors caused you to believe you were going the right direction when in reality you were lost?

- How long did you drive before you knew you were lost?

- While you were lost, did you remain confident that you were going in the right direction? How long did this period of confidence last? What began to erode your confidence and make you think you could be going in the wrong direction?

Now think about non-Christians you have known who were lost spiritually but did not know it. Consider the following questions:

- Where would your friends rank themselves on the following scale? Write the person's name above the number:

sure they   1_____2_____3_____4_____5   sure they
are not lost   are lost

Where would you rank your friends? Write the person's name under the number.

- What did your non-Christian friends say and do that expressed their confidence that they had nothing to worry about spiritually?

- What do you think causes non-Christians to move from being sure they are not lost spiritually to being less sure about their spiritual condition and say "I may be spiritually lost"?

COMING NEXT: NOT BY FORCE

As lostologists, we know people can be lost and not know it. But why not simply tell them, "Hey buddy, you're lost; admit it." Sounds good. Certainly it would be the truth. But this "in your face" approach violates the fifth law of lostology. Understanding this law helps us plot an alternate and hopefully more effective strategy of evangelism. We will learn more about this strategy in the next chapter.

Never Say Lost

> You stiff-necked people,
> with uncircumcised hearts and ears!
> You are just like your fathers:
> You always resist the Holy Spirit!
> Acts 7:51

Lostology Law #5
You cannot force people to admit they are lost.

Passengers in my car often accuse me of being lost. (Their accusations appear to have some connection with the fact that I do get lost so often.) My response is always controlled, appropriate, measured: "Lost? What do you mean 'lost'? I'm not lost!"

Still, they persist. Therefore, I have composed various explanations for why I often *appear* lost:

- "No, I don't think we just drove by that McDonalds. It may look like the same McDonalds to you, but I'm sure it isn't. Are you wearing your contacts?"

- "Lost? Me? I know I'm not lost. Frankly, I am a bit concerned about you. Do you have a problem with geographic disorientation?"

- "Oh no, I'm not lost. This is a short cut. You'll see. We'll save lots of time."

- "Stop and ask for directions? Totally unnecessary. There's no reason to do anything drastic. This is starting to look familiar to me."

- "Lost? Me? Lost? Are you accusing me of being an irresponsible driver? I don't mind telling you that I take that personally and I don't appreciate your attitude one little bit."

- "Driving in circles? I can't believe you'd say a thing like that. I assure you I know what I'm doing. But if you want to drive, I can stop this car right now and let you take over."

- "Lost?" Silence. "LOST?" Silence. "LOST?" Silence. "No, nothing's wrong. I just don't want to talk about it."

A SLAP IN THE FACE

How do you respond when someone suggests you are lost? How do you feel? Over the years, I have talked to lots of people, especially men, and all agree that it really irritates them when anyone suggests they are lost. I understand perfectly. Suggesting you are lost is a slap at your competence. If someone questions whether you can find your way, who knows what other areas of your life they will question next.

Key ⇒

HARD TRUTH FOR HARD HEARTS

When it comes to confronting people about being spiritually lost, I think about Jesus' encounter with the Pharisees. Remember these were veteran spiritual insiders—at least they thought so. Yet Jesus understood what they could not comprehend: they were spiritually lost. Subtle approaches did not work with these guys. Jesus preached sermons. He told stories. He met with them individually. Finally, when their opposition to His ministry reached a dangerous pitch, Jesus leveled the big guns at them. Here is a paraphrase of His encounter as recorded in Matthew 23:

- You are like a bunch of tombs filled with dead men's bones.

- You are like fancy cups, clean and shiny on the outside so you look good to others, but inside you are filthy.

- You think you are so spiritual that you travel all over seeking people to be proselytes. But when you convert people, you make them twice the sons of hell you are!

- You are like eye doctors, working to remove specks from patients' eyes while you have huge planks poking out of your eyes.

Pretty direct, don't you think? The Pharisees went ballistic. Although they needed every bit of Jesus' rebuke, they did not accept a word of it.

CONFUSED PRIORITIES

Jesus not only confronted the religious leaders of the day who were lost and did not know it, He dealt with other people he encountered.

One day, a rich, young man walked up to Jesus (see Mark 10). Even though Jesus was in the middle of a lesson, the self-absorbed young man interrupted. "Teacher," he asked, "what must I do to inherit eternal life?" Jesus responded, "You know the laws." The young man swelled out his chest in pride and said, "I've kept the laws my entire life."

Jesus was not impressed. Others might have mistaken this law-keeper for a super-saint but Jesus didn't. He recognized a lost soul.

Nothing short of spiritual shock treatment could bring this young man to his senses, so Jesus issued a high voltage blast to his heart. "Why don't you sell all you have and follow Me?" Jesus challenged the man. No response. The spiritual EKG showed a straight line. The rich young man turned and walked away, very sad and very lost.

Although Jesus loved the Pharisees and the rich young man with His incredible love, these encounters illustrate a basic principle of lostology: When people are lost and not ready to admit it, there is little anyone can do to force them to say, "I'm lost." *Jesus knew this*

TRUTH THAT IS HARD TO ADMIT

When I first envisioned the work of our new church in Portland, I pictured a church where thoughtful spiritual seekers would come, ask questions, hear the compelling logic of the gospel, and decide to trust Christ. Schooled in apologetics, I felt prepared to engage people in convicting conversation. "Give me a seeker," I thought, "and I'll lead him down the apologetic trail to Christ." Wrong.

Henry crushed my strategy. He was the ultimate salesman, an accomplished talker. Talking with him was like talking to an Einstein-level five-year-old. One question raised other questions; one string of logic became lost in another. With Henry, conversation was a game, an opportunity to pare mind against mind in a winner-take-all intellectual slugfest.

Henry had plenty of reasons to recognize his lost condition. Every circumstance and every relationship in his life called out to him, demanding that he face reality: his life was not working. He was spiritually lost and that condition impacted every area of his life. I really wanted Henry to acknowledge this foundational problem. Yet hard as I tried, I never made progress with him. He was lost, but he was still in the Lost Zone. I could point to the turn he had missed but until he sensed that reality, no amount of pushing created the desired effect. He refused to admit he was lost.

CLIMBING THE LADDER

While we cannot force secular people to admit they are lost, we can try to raise questions in their minds about their spiritual condition. Many non-Christians are overly optimistic about their relationship with God and are convinced they will fare well in any life to come. Without a biblical frame of reference, they set their own standards and easily pass their self-styled tests.

When talking to secular people about what it means to be right with God, it helps to give them a frame of reference. Pastor Bill Hybels of Willowcreek Community Church uses the following simple illustration. Draw a ladder on a piece of paper and explain that it represents the way we move toward God. God is at the top; people are at the bottom. Ask those you are talking with where they think they are on that ladder.

The Ladder illustration

Before they respond, give them a strong dose of perspective. Explain that if Billy Graham or Mother Theresa or any other famous spiritual person were asked where they ranked apart from Jesus Christ, these leaders would put themselves on one of the lower rungs. Mark an X on the ladder and write these famous Christians' names by the X. Then, for emphasis, make another X below these and write your name. Explain that on your own merits, you would rank far below these renowned spiritual leaders. Pause for a moment, then ask again where the non-Christians would rank themselves.

This is quite an adjustment for most people. It presents a different way of thinking about being lost. For most secular people, this simple ladder illustration raises enough doubts about their relationship with God to get them thinking about their spiritual lives—sometimes for the first time. This awareness will not lead them to Christ but it can be a positive step in the right direction. We cannot force people to admit they are lost.

Through asking questions, we help them think about spiritual issues. For a person in the inital stages of moving toward God, questioning your old ideas is a major step of progress.

THE LOSTOLOGY LAB

To help you identify with non-Christians who struggle to admit they are spiritually lost, recall a time when you were physically lost but refused to admit it:

- If you were alone, how long did it take you to admit to yourself that you were lost? If you were with other people, did you find it harder or easier to admit you were lost? Why?

- Why do you think it is so difficult for people, especially men, to admit they are lost?

Think about non-Christians you know who have struggled to admit they were spiritually lost. Now consider these questions:

- How did they respond once they learned what the Bible teaches about salvation and the fact that those without Christ are spiritually lost? Did they welcome this message or resist it? Why?

- In your conversations with non-Christians, have you ever tried to force them to admit they are spiritually lost? What happened? What did you learn?

- Do you find that it is harder for men than for women to admit they are spiritually lost? If so, why?

COMING NEXT: SEIZE THE MOMENT

You cannot force people to admit they are lost, but you can watch for the reality to dawn on them. It comes slowly, but when it comes, that is your opportunity. We will learn more about this important moment in the next chapter.

The Painful Truth

> When he [the prodigal son] came to his senses, he said,
> "How many of my father's hired men have food to spare,
> and here I am starving to death! I will set out
> and go back to my father . . . "
> Luke 15:17

Lostology Law #6
Admitting you are lost is the first step in the right direction.

The Children's Museum in Portland, Oregon, falls into the "You can't get there from here" category.

Even now, after repeated visits to this creative facility, I still struggle to find it. Tucked away in back streets off a confusing stretch of road, the Children's Museum presents a directional challenge to the navigational expert—much more to the directionally challenged.

I always went to this facility with a carload of kids. Usually the load included my two daughters, Courtney and Kelly, and their friends. My girls have known about my tendency to get lost since they were very young. They have learned to recognize the defense lines I use to explain the fact that we really are not lost. Such was the case on one memorable trip to the Children's Museum.

My girls were in the back seat with their friend Sarah. My wife, Lynn Marie, sat in front with me. We were trying to find the museum and needed to be there at the specific time for a special program. It was raining, dark, and cold outside. We wound our way around the general area in which the museum was located, attempting to accidentally stumble upon it.

I had told Lynn Marie and the girls I knew the way. Map in hand, I knew we were close. But try as I might, I could not find the street. Still, I would not admit defeat.

In frustration, the girls asked, "Daddy, are we lost again?" I grimaced. "No, girls. We're not lost. I know right where we are." Unsatisfied, they continued, "Are we going to miss the program?" Frustration mounted. "No. We're almost there. We won't miss the program."

Drive . . . Drive . . . Drive . . . "Mr. Kramp," Sarah said from the back seat, "I think you should have turned back there." That really galled me. Sarah was a first grader. I was not about to take directions from a first grader. "Thank you, Sarah," I said in my most controlled voice. "I know where to turn."

More wrong turns and dead ends. More questions from the back seat. Gentle exhortations from my wife to stop and ask direction. Finally, exasperated, I stopped the car and said:

"All right. We are now *officially* lost."

There, I said it. I said the "L" word. Dejected, embarrassed, I stopped and asked directions. The museum was two blocks over. Sarah, the first grader, had been right.

THE MOMENT OF TRUTH

It is humbling to be forced to admit we are lost. Pride must be swallowed; words must be eaten. The reality dawns that we blew it. Wrong turns and bad choices combined to get us lost. It is a clarifying moment. We stand defenseless facing the truth that we are lost, truly lost.

Women appear to handle these moments better than men. For men, these moments of truth are traumatic. I am not sure why this quirk in the male makeup exists. But whatever the reason, men steadfastly resist admitting they are lost. Yet even men cannot stay in the Lost Zone forever. The gnawing awareness grows until we say: "I really think I'm lost." Lostology Law #6 presents this truth but offers hope. An admission that we are lost is the first step we take in the right direction. This step is painful but essential if we have any hope of going home.

PIG PEN THERAPY

When Jesus told the story of the prodigal son, He described the young man's experience as he moved out on his own, lived the "fast life" on his family inheritance, and ultimately ended up feeding pigs when he ran out of funds. That young man, standing among the pigs, grew so hungry that he began to look with longing at the slop the pigs ate. For him, that longing was the jolt that brought him to a decision. He admitted he was *officially* lost. Pig pens were not the place for him. He was born for something more. In his father's home, even if he were a slave, he would not dine with pigs.

Jesus described that point in the young man's life as the time when he "came to his senses." How appropriate. Out of the fog of confusion, the clouds parted and the young man saw the navigational stars. He stepped out of his experience and said, "What has become of me?" More than that, he examined his choices. Would he stay with the pigs? Or would he take that first step out of the pig pen and begin the long walk home? All who know the story, know the choice he made. With one decision and one step, he changed the course of his life.

ADMITTING THE TRUTH

We were closing the worship service in our church. My sermon that morning addressed several truths that had strong application for the seekers among us. Knowing we had a number of individuals who needed to deal seriously with their spiritual lives, I called for a step of commitment.

In the crowd that morning was a man named Phil. More than most who attended our church, Phil resisted the gospel and refused to admit he was lost. But that morning, he seemed especially focused on what I was saying.

While others had their eyes closed, I asked those who knew they were not Christians but who were ready to follow Christ to raise their hands. I waited and watched, focusing especially on Phil.

Up to that point, his hands had been in his lap. I watched as he crossed his arms. In a few seconds, his right hand moved to his chin where it paused as if he needed to scratch. Then his hand moved to the right of his head. *Great*, I thought, *he is about to raise his hand.* I kept watching, but he moved his hand behind his head and smoothed down his hair. Still I watched and waited. In a few more moments, Phil slowly raised his hand above his head and held it there for me to see. He was admitting to me, and to himself, that he was lost.

I will never forget Phil and the process he went through that morning. His struggle to admit he was lost confirms the reality of Lostology Law #6. It *is* difficult for people to admit they have been going in the wrong direction. Yet once they step over that line and admit they are lost, something fundamental changes in their lives. The future opens wide before them. Changes become possible.

GENTLE DOES IT

Evangelism becomes more productive when people move out of the Lost Zone and into the coming-to-their-senses phase. Lostologists learn to watch for signs that indicate people are beginning to admit they are lost. Here are a few indicators to watch for:

- an interest in reading the Bible or Christian literature

- questions about spiritual matters and about what Christians believe

- an interest in attending church

- expressions of dissatisfaction with the direction they have been going in life

- wishful longing for a chance to start over in life

- regrets over decisions made in the past

Good indicators

But what about those who are not ready to admit they are lost? What do we do with them? How hard do we push to get them to see how much they need God?

I am convinced there is nothing I can do to convict people of sin or to convince them they are lost. I continue to talk to them about Christ and explain what the Bible says about how to have a relationship with Jesus. But beyond that, I don't push. It is not that I don't care about people and long for them to trust Christ. I have just learned that I cannot do God's work. Conviction of sin is His responsibility. He works in His time. God directs the affairs of people's lives so they find themselves in an environment that heightens the awareness that their lives are not working. When people stand in pig slop and long to go home, sharing the gospel becomes easy.

The Lostology Lab

In this lab session, we will work with the following case study:

Imagine you are traveling interstate highway on your way to an important meeting. Unfortunately, you missed a turn and are on the wrong highway. For several miles, you have been driving in the wrong direction without knowing you were lost.

Gradually you start to feel that things "don't look right." You begin to wonder if you are going in the right direction. A sign indicates you are one mile from an exit leading to service stations and restaurants where you can ask directions. The same sign states that if you do not take the next exit, you will have to drive twenty-seven miles to find additional service stations and restaurants.

Lostology Law #6 states that "Admitting you are lost is the first step in the right direction." Apply law #6 to this case study by answering the following questions and making application to what non-Christians feel as they struggle to admit they are spiritually lost:

- In the situation described in this case study, would you stop and ask directions at the next exit or keep driving? What considerations would lead you to stop? What considerations would lead you to keep driving?

- Let's assume you pull off the highway to look at your map. You have not changed your direction, but at least you are not moving further away from where you need to be. In what ways do non-Christians make a "pull-off-the-road-and-think-about-it" decision concerning their spiritual lives? How is this decision different from admitting they are spiritually lost and asking for spiritual directions?

- Let's pretend that while you are looking at your map, you say "I don't know how it happened, but I'm not where I'm supposed to be; I'm lost." What is the value of that admission? What are the consequences of that admission? How does this apply to non-Christians who admit they are lost? Why is their admission the first step in the right direction?

COMING NEXT: NO MORE OPTIONS

Once people admit to themselves they are lost, they take a small step in the right direction. But lostologists understand the first step is usually tiny and tentative. In most cases, that first step leads to an intermediate step before the person finds the right road home—a stop to ask directions.

PART TWO

When All Else Fails, Ask Directions

Lost Control

But the way of the wicked is like deep darkness;
they do not know what makes them stumble.

Proverbs 4:19

Lostology Law #7
When you are lost, you are out of control.

The summer heat of 1987 spawned a frightening phenomenon in Los Angeles: freeway shootings. Frustrated with life, people started shooting each other from their cars. Drivers feared they would get shot going to work or to the grocery store. The situation grew increasingly tense. The network news told the story to the nation. In the middle of it all, I boarded a plane heading to Los Angeles.

The trip had been planned for months; there was no way to change it. When I landed at the L.A. airport that summer, I had one central goal—don't get shot! My strategy was simple: drive in such a way that I didn't irritate anyone. Sounded good. The problem was David. I barely knew him and knew nothing about his strange gift.

David Palmer was a church planting expert who was working with me to begin our new church in Oregon. We had been together briefly a few months earlier before we met in L.A. to continue our planning. While we waited for our rental car, I asked, "Do you know how to get where we're going?" David nodded with confidence and said, "Sure. I'll navigate; you drive." Relieved to have someone who knew his way around Los Angeles, I agreed and we loaded up the car. Big mistake.

Heading out of the airport, I began getting nervous. My one consolation was that David was navigating and David knew the way. We traveled down a mammoth, multi-lane strip of freeway. "Which way do we turn?" I asked as we headed into a section where the highway branched off in multiple directions. David looked around, shook his head, but said nothing. The turn grew closer. Suddenly he pointed to the right then blurted out, "There. Right lane. Get in the right lane." Instinctively, I swerved across four lanes, barely negotiating the turn as horns blared. "Are you sure you know where we're going?" I asked as doubt crept in. "Trust me," David said.

Moments later we began to see signs indicating another set of choices to be made. "Which way now?" I asked. Again, silence. At the last minute, David pointed left then yelled, "Left. Left. You've got to go left." Once again, instincts kicked in and I shot through a break in the traffic, slicing my way to the turn at the last minute. "What's the deal?" I shouted at David. "I thought you knew your way around here?" David smiled and said, "I do . . . sort of." "What do you mean, 'sort of'?" I retorted.

At this point, I hesitate to tell you what he said because you will think I am making this up. You will just have to trust me. David admitted that he had only driven *around* L.A. in the past and had not really driven *through* the city. He told me not to worry, however, because he had a special gift, a gift of directions. With this gift he could sense directional auras in an area and follow the auras to his destination.

Sensing my disbelief, he launched into a long story about a time he had gone to San Francisco to meet with the leaders of a group of Chinese people who had come to America and wanted to start a new church in Portland. David explained that he did not know exactly where to find the people so he just drove around following the auras. After a while, sensing he was in aura-alignment, he stopped at a phone booth and called. Surprise, surprise, he was one block from their home. That settled it for him, he had the gift. David was convinced.

I, too, was convinced—absolutely convinced he was crazy! At that point I did not know David well and knew nothing of his reputation as a practical joker. I took him at face value—he was a mental case. So there I was, totally lost, driving through L.A. about to get shot because of a crazy man navigating by auras! Talk about a loss of control.

OUT OF CONTROL

Why do we dislike being lost? Think back on some of the times you have been lost. Why did you respond as you did in that situation? What did you fear? Why did you hesitate to ask for help or directions?

The central drive that fuels our emotions when we are lost is control. We like to be in control of our lives. We like to drive our own cars, listen to our own music, follow our own schedules. We crave control. We dislike being vulnerable.

In her book, *The Popcorn Report*, social researcher Faith Popcorn describes a phenomenon of our day she calls "cocooning." She explains it this way:

> We defined cocooning when we named it as the impulse to go *inside* when it gets too tough and scary *outside*. To pull a shell of safety around yourself, so you're not at the mercy of a mean, unpredictable world . . . Cocooning is about insulation and avoidance, peace and protection, coziness and control.[3]

{ Cocooning

We have become fearful people. The problem is we are also needy people so we cannot cocoon forever. In reality, we cannot control our environments and are inherently vulnerable. How hard we work to deny this reality. All the same, we reach points in life where we cannot continue alone. We need help from others. This need creates a crisis for us. With need comes a loss of control. Need shatters our illusion of self-sufficiency. Gone is the notion that we can draw into our cocoons and watch life through a peep hole.

NO OPTIONS, NO CONTROL

In the story of the prodigal son, the lost boy ultimately reached the point where he had no options except to go home. His self-styled cocoon burst and he found himself feeding pigs. With the decision to go home, the boy gave up control of his life. He became vulnerable. He could not dictate how his father would respond to him. In fact, he constructed a worst-case-scenario of how his father would react:

> I will set out and go back to my father and say to him: "Father, I have sinned against heaven and against you. I am no longer worthy to be called your son; make me like one of your hired men." (Luke 15:18-19)

He envisioned life as a slave in his father's house. Not an especially appealing option. Of course, he was not exactly flush with alternatives.

Where he was, he had no control; he was lost in a pig pen, hungry and desperate. Certainly, in reaching out to his father he had no control but at least the circumstances could change for the better. They certainly could not get worse.

STRIVING FOR CONTROL

There is nothing like limited options to clarify some of life's issues. Unfortunately, most lost people do not seek God until they run out of options. Even then, they often cling to control in any way possible.

When new people visited our church in Portland, it was always easy to spot them. They usually:

- came into the service late

- sat at the back

- did not complete registration cards

- slipped out the door during the closing prayer

For a while, I observed but did not understand this phenomenon. As I talked to some of the folks who came back after an initial visit and early exit, I began to understand more. They were attempting to control as much of their environments as possible.

Their lives overall were already out of control; that was why they visited church in the first place. But the struggle to maintain control was intense. Given any opportunity at all, they tried to get the help they needed without giving up control. For secular adults who had never gone to church, attending a service proved to be an unnerving experience and they looked for ways of escape if they became uncomfortable.

EASING FEAR FOR LOST FRIENDS

When people begin to sense they are spiritually lost, they experience emotional turmoil because they feel vulnerable. Who can blame them; there are plenty of religious crazies out there. Who can a person trust?

It is easy for us to say "trust us." In our church settings, we are comfortable and relaxed. We know what to do, what to say, how to dress, how to act. We know the people around us and trust them. It is easy to forget that for a newcomer, especially a spiritual seeker, a church full of strangers can be an intimidating situation.

We can help seekers take these initial steps that seem so difficult for them. By recognizing their feelings of vulnerability and moving with sensitivity to help them find a new set of spiritual directions, we can help. That is where our perspective as lostologists becomes valuable. Drawing on our past experiences in being lost, we can recall how we felt when we were lost. We can remember the frustration, the fear, the loss of control. From there, we can easily transfer our insights to our secular friends and relate to how they feel as they search for spiritual answers. It is one way we can get "in their shoes."

Here are a few guidelines that can help:

- Give people emotional space and time. Give them time to open up. Do not push or pry. If you have invited them to join you at your church, allow them to be anonymous spectators with others if that is what they want.

- Allow people to tell you about themselves in stages. Give trust time to grow. Open your life to them and they will feel more comfortable opening their lives to you. Be patient. Allow them to set the pace.

- Minimize situations that make seekers stand out from the group and make them feel odd or unusual. Help them blend in to the group, to feel welcome and not different.

Pastor Bill Hybels says that seekers have specific goals when they attend church initially—they do not want to sing anything, say anything, sign anything, or give anything. That is just another way of saying they want to watch from a safe distance until they are comfortable. Seekers struggle with loss of control. If we push too hard or attempt to rush them, we may find they leave and never come back.

THE LOSTOLOGY LAB

- There are many reasons we dislike being lost. What are some of your reasons?

- What do you want to control that you cannot control when you are lost?

- How do you attempt to compensate for your loss of control when you're lost? In what ways do you try to minimize your loss of control?

Imagine that you have been trying to share your faith with a neighbor who is involved in a large New Age church in your city. Your neighbor is open to the gospel but asks you to attend his church with him. Reluctantly, you agree to attend a service with him the following Sunday. What would you be thinking and feeling as you headed to the New Age church service?

- Would you drive your own car or meet your friend at the church? Why?

- Would you arrive early, right on time, or just after the service started? Why?

- Would you want to wear a name tag? Why?

- Would you want to introduce yourself to the people seated around you? Why?

- Would you want to stand up and introduce yourself to the congregation? Why?

- Would you leave your children with the childcare workers at the church? Why?

- Would you want the church to have a printed order of service? Why?

- Would you want to sing the songs the church used in the service? Why?

- Would you complete a registration card? Why?

- Would you give any money at the offering time? Why?

- Would you want to talk with the pastor as you left the service? Why?

- Would you want someone from the church to visit you? Why?

Now, think about non-Christian friends you have invited to attend church with you. Recall how they responded to your invitation:

- What did they do and say? Why do you think they responded as they did? Evaluate their responses in light of how you think you would respond if you were invited to attend the New Age church.

- What did their responses tell you about their fears and their desire to control their environments?

- Because of what you are learning about lostology, what will you do next time you invite a non-Christian friend to attend church with you?

COMING NEXT: AN IMPORTANT DISTINCTION

Being lost not only makes you feel vulnerable, it makes you feel stupid. Well, that is not exactly right. You do not feel stupid, but you are afraid others think you are stupid. We will probe this confusing situation in the next chapter.

Lost . . . Not Stupid

When Jesus reached the spot,
he looked up [in the sycamore tree] and said,
"Zacchaeus, come down immediately.
I must stay at your house today.
So he came down at once and welcomed him gladly.
Luke 19:5-6

Lostology Law #8
Just because you are lost does not mean you are stupid.

A strange, recurring nightmare plagues me. I am driving a rental car in a
ghetto area of a large city. Windowless buildings hover high above creating
a canopy of darkness. I have no idea how I got there. Powerful emotions
grip me, squeezing my chest until I struggle to breathe. Desperately, I look
for a landmark—something to get me back on the right track. Nothing.
I look for a gas station, a convenience store, any place I can stop and ask
directions. Nothing. Then, off to one side of the street, I see a large, vacant
lot. Toward the front of the lot is a small building. Above the building is
a sign: "Bubba's Fill Dirt and Espresso." I question the wisdom of stopping,
but given my options, I pull the car in front, get out, and cautiously step
inside.

There, standing behind a crude espresso bar is Bubba, a lifesize, living
character right out of one of Gary Larson's "Far Side" cartoons. He grins
a twisted, toothless smile and says, "Espresso or fill dirt?" "Neither," I say.
"Just directions."

With that, Bubba lets out a shrill, heckling laugh. "Directions? Did you say directions?" As he talks, he jumps up and down behind the espresso bar. "Sure I can give you directions," he says. "But first you'll have to do something."

Fearfully, I ask, "What?" Bubba smiles a sick smile as he pops the straps of his overalls, then responds, "See that sign and that hat over there?" He points to the corner where a large, cone-shaped dunce cap rests on a tattered stool. Leaning against the stool is a bright orange sign with florescent lime-green letters painted on it. "Pick it up," Bubba says. "Pick up the sign and put on the hat." Reluctantly, I walk to the corner, pick up the hat and look at it. In vertical letters, the hat reads, "I'm stupid." I lean over and pick up the sign. In scrawled letters it reads, "I'm lost." Bubba begins to dance around wildly. "Put on the hat and hold the sign. Stand outside. Stand there 'til I say stop then I'll give you directions."

For some reason, I pick up the "I'm stupid" hat and place it on my head. I grasp the "I'm lost" sign and hold it in front of me as I walk out the door. As I move toward the street, a crowd gathers, laughing and jeering at me. Bubba bounds out the door shouting like a barker at a carnival: "That's right, folks. Step right up. See him while you can. He's lost and he's stupid." The crowd presses in around me. Only it is not a crowd of people; it is a mob of "Far Side" characters—cows, amoebas, insects, and other bizarre figures pushing and shoving. As the mob presses around me, they begin to chant with growing intensity, "Lost and stupid. Lost and stupid. Lost and stupid." On and on the chant continues. "No, I protest. I'm not stupid. I'm just lost." But to no avail. The "Far Side" voices drown out my one voice. "Lost and stupid. Lost and stupid. Lost and . . . " That is when I wake up.

Not Just a Bad Dream

All right, so I made up the dream. But I have still experienced the emotions of that dream in real life. Have you ever felt that way? Be honest now. When you have stopped to ask directions, didn't you have the feeling people were snickering at you and saying, "Look at her, Madelle. She's lost. She's probably stupid, too."

There are some direction-givers who enjoy the power that comes with having a lost person wait for help. They say, "You'll have to wait until I defrost the freezer in the back of the store." Or, "I'll help you as soon as I rebuild the engine on this car."

In most cases, however, those giving directions do not intend to make the lost person feel stupid. All the same, a condescending expression, a side-glance and grin at another worker can give the impression that only a stupid person could get lost like you are lost.

In reality, feeling stupid probably has more to do with how the lost person feels than with what the direction-giver intends to communicate. It is embarrassing to ask for directions. We already feel silly, possibly stupid. Anything others do only adds to that feeling.

A STUDY IN SENSITIVITY

When lost people came to Jesus, He never made them feel stupid:

- Think of Zachaeus up the sycamore tree (see Luke 19). Picture the wee little tax collector peeking through a clump of leaves. What a setup for making someone feel stupid. But Jesus did not belittle him. In fact, he honored him. In front of the crowd, Jesus said, "Zachaeus, come on down. I'd like to have lunch at your house today."

- How about the woman caught in adultery, brought to Jesus by a group of men seeking to trap him and stone her (see John 8). Imagine her fear, her embarrassment, her humiliation. But Jesus, the master of the moment, stooped down to write in the dirt. Every eye turned to Him. He stood and said, "I'll tell you what. Go ahead and stone her, but here are the rules. The one who has never sinned . . . let him throw the first rock." The crowd left. Jesus stood alone with the woman. What would He say? Would He give her a lecture? Would He scold her, rebuke her? No, He simply said, Woman, where are your accusers?" "There are none," she replied. "Neither do I accuse you," Jesus said. "Go and don't live this way any more."

What an incredible way to relate to lost people. At every point, Jesus dealt with people in a way that allowed them to sense His love and understand that He valued them as people. They were lost, but they were not stupid.

EXPERTS IN DIFFERENT AREAS

When adults without religious background begin their spiritual searches, they lack many of the conceptual building blocks for spiritual under-standing. They do not know the stories first graders in Sunday School have already mastered. Many decide to read the Bible, begin with the first chapter of Genesis, and die in Leviticus—if they get that far. Christians talk to them in a mixture of church jargon and biblical references. Feeling lost and stupid become major obstacles for these seekers.

Sheila was this kind of seeker. To protect her from frustration as she inched her way into a new world of church and spiritual discussions, I asked her about her professional life as a financial planner. We discussed the scope of concepts she had mastered as she progressed in her career. She told me about the struggles she faced daily as she communicated financial information to her clients.

I explained that if I wanted to learn more about financial planning, I would struggle initially—not because I am stupid but because I am not oriented. Brokers could make me feel stupid by not taking time to explain concepts or by using professional jargon. Yet that would reflect poorly on them, not me.

As Sheila and I continued to discuss her growing faith, she understood that I related to her as she related to her clients. Drawing on my knowledge, skills, and experience, I provided an orientation for her in the same way she drew on her knowledge, skills, and experience to help her clients. This understanding framed our discussions and helped us discuss and share in ways that made Sheila feel at ease . . . and never stupid.

CHECK YOUR ASSUMPTIONS

We need to approach people with the assumption that they are intelligent people who simply have not been exposed to spiritual truths. As you move into discussions about spiritual things, consider these steps:

- Discover the areas in which people excel, whether these areas are in their professional lives or even in their hobbies. Everyone is good at something. Find it and affirm it.

- Acknowledge that there are many areas in which you have lim-ited knowledge and must rely on those with expertise to help you grow in understanding. If the people you are talking with have special expertise in particular areas, affirm that you can learn much from them.

- Explain that once you share what the Bible has to say about how people relate to God, they will understand it. Tell them that spiritual truths are not difficult to understand. Initially, it may be confusing but that is simply because the information is new.

- Tell seekers you know they are highly capable, intelligent people who can evaluate ideas and make appropriate decisions.

Some Christians do great damage as they relate to seekers because of their own insecurities. Sensing that they know more than the lost person, they strut their biblical knowledge. Seekers are not impressed by those who are impressed with themselves. Much more will be accomplished by sharing naturally what you know about spiritual matters without pretending that you know everything. Your weaknesses can actually become a strength. If your seeker friends sense you are still growing and learning, they will be more comfortable beginning their own spiritual journeys. In all you say and do, communicate that you recognize the difference between being lost and being stupid.

The Lostology Lab

- How do you feel when you get lost and must stop and ask directions?

- Are you concerned you may appear foolish because you are lost? If so, how do you attempt to compensate for these feelings when you ask for directions?

- In what ways do direction-givers unintentionally make lost people feel stupid? What do the direction-givers do? What do they say?

- In your interaction with spiritual seekers, what do they say or do that lets you know they are concerned about appearing foolish or stupid?

- What do Christians do unintentionally that makes spiritual seekers feel more self-conscious or even stupid?

- What can Christians do to help spiritual seekers feel more at ease and comfortable as they interact in a Christian setting?

Coming Next: Strangers Among Us

A by-product of our sick society is that parents must warn their children to beware of strangers. We learn to evaluate people and determine if they pose a threat to us. Is it any wonder we struggle to choose a stranger to ask directions when we are lost? Overcoming this struggle is a focus in lostology and the subject of the next chapter.

Stranger Danger

Many of the Samaritans from that town
believed in him [Jesus] because of the woman's testimony,
"He told me everything I ever did."
. . . And because of her words many more became believers.
John 4:39-41

Lostology Law #9
It is tough to trust a stranger.

I heard him coming long before I saw him. I was washing my hands in
the church restroom when his loud, high-pitched voice bounced around
the corner and reverberated off the tiles. As he entered the room, he banged
the metal door for good measure and continued singing full blast. He
rounded the corner, racing for his destination.

As he came 'round the tile wall behind the door, he saw me. Silence.
Frozen kid. There he stood, about five years old, shorts, t-shirt, freckled
face—a boy I had never seen before. He stared at me, unsure of what to
do or say. What a dilemma. From the speed with which he entered the
restroom, he was obviously on an urgent mission. My presence complicated matters. Amused, but not showing it, I stared back at him without
saying a word.

After a moment, he shifted his weight, put his hands on his hips, pulled
himself up to his most intimidating height, looked me square in the eyes
and demanded, "Are you a stranger?" The question hung in the air. I
waited, matching his intense gaze. "No," I replied without emotion. He

nodded his head, gave me one more examining look, then simply said, "That's good." And with that he raced past me into one of the restroom stalls.

CHOOSING YOUR STRANGER

Strangers are complicated people. Ask any kid who has been through *stranger-danger* training in school. There are good strangers and rotten strangers and it is tough to tell one from the other. Who can you trust? If you are lost and need directions, what type of stranger do you talk to?

- strangers in gas stations or in convenience stores?

- strangers in fast food restaurants or strangers on the street?

- men strangers or women strangers?

- younger strangers or older strangers?

- boss strangers or worker strangers?

- busy strangers or strangers just standing around?

Most of us go through this stranger-selection process without realizing the complicated decision making we are doing. As lostologists, we must become aware of what we feel in these situations and the decisions we make. What we learn can provide helpful insights into how we relate to spiritual seekers.

If there are no other options, we will seek help from strangers. That does not mean we like it. The world is filled with crazy people. How do we know the stranger we ask will help rather than hurt us. He could be an ax-murderer working part-time at the convenience store or an escapee from the mental ward cooking hamburgers. Perhaps the stranger we talk to will give us the wrong directions. Who says he knows more about the area than we do? Dealing with strangers is an intimidating business.

STARTING WITH FRIENDS

Is it any wonder we prefer to talk with someone we know when we need help? That is why we stop at a pay phone and call a friend to ask directions rather than talk to the mechanic at the service station. We will drop by a friend's house and ask directions before we will stop at the local Burger

King and admit to a teenager cashier that we are lost. Only when we are out of friends do we turn to strangers. Even then, we don't like it.

The ninth law of lostology builds on this experience and applies it to evangelism. This laws states: It is tough to trust a stranger. When seekers recognize their need for spiritual directions, they don't know who to talk with and where to seek help. Most secular people do not have close Christian friends who can answer their questions or recommend a church. So what are their alternatives?

If their current situation creates enough pressure in their lives, they may venture out alone in search of spiritual answers. Some Sunday, they may show up at a church they have heard about or seen. They may even call a church office and ask to speak with the pastor. These steps require a great deal of initiative and a willingness to take risks—more initiative and risk than many seekers are willing to take.

Seekers want to turn to people they know. They think through their circle of friends and acquaintances and try to identify someone who is "into religion." Perhaps it is simply someone who has mentioned attending church. Perhaps the friend is someone who has attempted to share her faith with the seeker in the past. Only now, confronted with new problems and pressures, the seeker is highly receptive. Sensitive Christians recognize how much a friend is needed at this critical time. Seekers need someone they can trust, possibly even someone who can introduce them to others who can help them find answers.

JESUS: THE INTRIGUING STRANGER

It is interesting how people entered into relationships with Jesus. Many encountered Him on their own with no previous introduction; they simply took the leap and trusted Him. But many others came to Jesus on the testimony and introduction of someone they knew.

On one occasion, Jesus encountered an outcast Samaritan woman at a well on the outskirts of her town (see John 4). When Jesus tried to talk with her—an unbelievable breach of etiquette for that day—she was appropriately guarded. But Jesus, the master relationship builder, gently guided her into a conversation using an intriguing series of questions and statements.

First Jesus asked, "Will you give me a drink?" This allowed him to talk to her about the well, the water, and being thirsty. Jesus then said, "If you knew the gift of God and who it is that asks you for a drink, you would have asked him and he would have given you living water." This captured the woman's attention.

Then Jesus changed the subject to her husband. "Go," Jesus said, "call your husband and come back." He knew she had already had five husbands and was currently living with a man. His statement touched the deepest hurts and fears in her life.

Overcome by the discussion, the woman said, "I know that the Messiah is coming. When he comes, he will explain everything to us." Jesus said to her, "I who speak to you am he."

Jesus captured her attention and touched her heart. In the end, she believed that He was the promised messiah. She found her trustworthy stranger.

The woman met Jesus alone; no one opened the way for her initial contact with Him. But the encounter was so powerful that she ran back into town and told everyone about the man she had met. On the strength of her testimony, the entire town headed out to meet Jesus. Her encounter helped others trust Jesus. She built a bridge for them to cross.

THE BRIDGE OF FRIENDSHIP

Secular people usually come to Christ over bridges of friendships. A trusted friend helps the seeker ease into a church and learn about Christ.

Sarah, one of the most memorable seekers to find Christ at Westside, was a bridge builder. She used her warm way with people to invite her friends and coworkers to come to our church. Paul was one who came. When she brought him, she made a special point to introduce him to me. He was open and receptive from our first encounter.

I found out later that Sarah had been telling Paul about me and our church for some time. Initially he was reluctant, but circumstances in his life changed and he eventually agreed to attend a service. In time, Paul and I became friends. That friendship led to wonderful conversations about what it means to become a Christian. His journey to Christ took months, but finally he completed that journey. A few months after I left Westside, Paul became a Christian—the fruit of the seeds Sarah planted in his life months before.

I never would have had that relationship with Paul if Sarah had not helped. He was open to me because Sarah prepared him to be open. Through her, I became a trustworthy stranger and had the chance to help

Paul find Christ. Sarah built the bridge to me; I built the bridge to Christ. Paul walked across.

Intentional Bridge Building

Few seekers are ready to trust Christ the first time they hear the gospel. It is difficult for adults to reverse a lifetime of beliefs and values on the basis of a one-shot presentation of spiritual truth. Certainly it happens, but I have learned not to count on it.

In Portland we helped seekers by inviting them to become part of our church family, not as members, but as people who shared our life together. As a group, we worked to become friends, not strangers to these people.

In that network of friendship, we exposed our new friends to the message of Christ in multiple ways. We invited them to worship with us, to work with us, to fellowship with us. We welcomed their questions. When we had church business meetings, we asked them to attend. We opened our lives to them so they could see the reality of our faith in the way we lived and related to each other. Before they could receive the message of Christ from us, they had to trust us. This took time. But it was worth all the time it took.

Bridge Building Steps

The most effective way to reach people for Christ is for Christians to work together and build bridges of relationships. Sometimes this happens spontaneously. More often, it is intentional. Here are a few practical steps you can take to build relationships with spiritual seekers:

- If you are a new Christian, you probably know many non-Christians. Introduce your friends and family members to some Christian friends or to your pastor. Try to connect people who share things in common. Look for natural, casual settings such as parties or social gatherings and let people get acquainted. If the relationship develops, fine. If not, do not push it. Keep watching for a match that works.

- If you are a Christian with few non-Christian friends, work with the newer Christians in your church. Get to know their friends and family members. Plan informal social gatherings together. Invite the new members and their friends to a party at your home, or meet for lunch one day. Watch for opportunities to nurture relationships with these people. For many longtime Christians, this is one of the best ways to broaden contacts with secular people.

As Christians seeking to reach secular people, we must be willing to give them time to consider following Christ. We must build friendships and nurture relationships. The ninth law of lostology reminds us that it is tough for them to trust a stranger. Knowing this, we take time and build trust. This is the best way to overcome "stranger danger."

THE LOSTOLOGY LAB

- When you are lost, do you prefer to ask directions from someone you know rather than from a stranger? Why?

- When you are lost, where do you stop to ask directions? Why?

- When you stop, with what type of person do you prefer to talk? Why?

- Since many non-Christians do not have close friends who are Christians, who will they talk with when they begin to search for spiritual answers?

- Do you know a non-Christian who came as a total stranger to your church? Why did he come to your church? What happened?

- Why is it important for Christians to work together and build relationships with non-Christians?

- What strategies have you used to build relationships with non-Christians? What have you done to introduce your non-Christian friends to other Christians? How have you developed relationships with non-Christians who are friends with someone you know?

COMING NEXT: DON'T MISS THE SIGNS

What signs indicate that someone is considering an important spiritual decision? Pay attention. They are so subtle, you may miss them. As a lostologist, you cannot allow that to happen. The next chapter will help you spot the signals seekers give when they are ready to begin a spiritual search.

There's More to the Question

Now a man came up to Jesus and asked,
"Teacher, what good thing must I do
to get eternal life?"
Matthew 19:16

Lostology Law #10
People ask for directions without revealing their true emotions.

When I ask directions, I am calm and controlled. "Excuse me," I say. "Can you tell me how to get to Bucksnort, Tennessee?" I smile, listen intently, say thank you, then get back in my car and drive away. "My, wasn't he calm and controlled," people say as I leave. (Actually, I don't know if they say that or not, but they should!) If they only knew. My calm outer self masks a smoldering volcano of emotions. Here's why:

- First, I never stop and ask directions until I have absolutely no other options. Therefore, by the time I stop, frustration has been building for a long time.

- Second, I never stop for directions, even if I have no options unless there is an important place I need to be. I just continue to drive around indefinitely. The fact that I stop for directions indicates that I am not only *lost*, but I am *late*.

- Third, the fact that I am asking directions is a sure sign that someone is in the car with me. In all but the rarest of situations, even if I am lost and need to be somewhere important, I refuse to stop and ask directions unless someone in the car with me—generally someone related to me by birth or marriage—is badgering me to stop.

So as I calmly request directions, don't be fooled—It is a cover-up. I am close to an emotional breaking point brought on by a combination of nagging and frustration. My question may *sound* calm and controlled. I may *appear* calm and controlled. I am not. In reality, I am in crisis. My emotions are raging torrents threatening to break out of their banks and wash away all in their midst.

Don't push me when I am in this emotional state. Don't make me wait in line. Don't even think about giving me a condescending look. I may erupt. Like Mount Saint Helens, I may spew emotional lava over everything. Don't be fooled by the surface-level question; there is more to it. The fact that I ask the question is serious business to me. Don't miss it. Don't underestimate it.

JUST BELOW THE SURFACE

Think back on the times you have stopped and asked directions. Picture yourself standing in that gas station talking with a mechanic. Remember him? What did he see when he looked at you? How would he describe you?

- Did you drop to your knees and cling to his leg begging him to tell you how to find the intersection of Main and Elm streets?

- Did you lay your head down on his tool box and sob uncontrollably?

- Did you grab him around the neck in a choke hold and shake his head side to side saying: "This is it, buddy. Give me directions. I'm desperate."

No way. You tried to look cool and calm. You probably did not wait as long as I did before you stopped, but you were still stretched emotionally. The question you asked masked the emotions you felt. That mechanic may have mistakenly assumed that since you looked calm and your question was controlled, you were really all right. Wrong. Your question did not tell the whole story.

PEEKING BEHIND THE STATEMENT

Jesus always tuned in to the people He met. He listened to their questions and even noticed what was not said, discerning the underlying issues.

One night, a spiritual bigwig came to Jesus (see John 3). Nicodemus was a leader among the Pharisees, and he was reluctant to let his powerful friends know he was talking to Jesus, the back woods Messiah. Therefore, he came at night so he could talk to Jesus alone. Nicodemus began the conversation with what he intended as a compliment:

> Rabbi, we know you are a teacher who has come from God. For no one could perform the miraculous signs you are doing if God were not with him. (John 3:2)

Good start. An ordinary person could have missed the significance of the statement but not Jesus. He knew it was a smoke screen for a man desperately seeking God:

> In reply Jesus declared, "I tell you the truth, unless a man is born again, he cannot see the kingdom of God." (John 3:3)

Boom! Straight for the spiritual jugular. No messing around here. Jesus knew this man was on a mission. Nicodemus was lost and asking for directions. Jesus wanted him to have all he came for, plus more. Jesus wanted him to be born again.

SUNDAY MORNING SIGNALS

It was a very big deal when a seeker showed up for services at our church in Portland. I did not understand the significance at first. Over time, I discovered that no seeker wakes up on Sunday morning and casually says, "I don't think I'll go to the coast or the mountains today. Church sounds good. That's what I'll do; I'll go to church."

No, if seekers walked in the door, something was going on. Usually, they were reacting to a crisis in their lives—a troubled marriage, problems with their kids, problems at work, some personal issue. Coming to church once . . . that was an important indicator. Coming to a service the second time . . . that was a sure sign God was at work in their lives.

Not only was church attendance a sign of awakening spiritual interest, but requests to "get together" became another indicator. It was amusing, how most people brought up the subject. "Would you like to get together sometime?" they would ask. "No big deal. I just had a couple of things I wanted to talk with you about."

Calm, collected questions and comments. I could have missed the emotions lurking beneath the surface, but I learned to recognize them. When we did get together, they would dump their entire emotional truck on me revealing the full range of issues that drove them to this point in their lives. How tragic if I had said, "I'm sorry. This is a busy time for me. Can we get together next month?" More than likely, there would not have been a next month. The opportunity would have been lost.

SENSITIVE TO THE SIGNALS

Many Christians miss the signals from seekers. We do not intend to miss them. We are simply not sensitized to the subtle ways seekers ask for help. Here are a few examples:

- Christians in an adult sunday school class visit together, eating donuts and drinking coffee, while a seeker couple sits alone, waiting for class to start. The Christians miss the significance of the seekers' presence. Fellowship among the Christians crowds out time for interaction with a new couple tentatively searching for spiritual answers.

- During conversation, a seeker may ask a question about the Bible or about church. Often, Christians dismiss the question as small talk and fail to probe for what is on the person's mind. Other times, Christians feel uncomfortable or ill-prepared to talk about spiritual matters. How tragic. What they know, as inadequate as it may be, could be just what the seeker needs to hear.

- A co-worker may ask where a Christian attends church. The Christian answers without recognizing that the question may indicate an interest in attending church. More than that, the seeker may be looking for an invitation to attend a particular church. Often Christians miss these opportunities because they do not want to appear pushy.

A SIGNAL SAMPLER

When seekers take a step of action in their spiritual searches, they do not carry a sign that says: "Don't miss me. I'm ready to talk about God."

Usually, their signals are subtle. Assume that if any of the following things happen, a seeker is signaling spiritual interest:

- *The Question Signal:* Pay attention to any question that has anything to do with spiritual matters. Seekers do not ask questions about the Bible or about attending church because they are suddenly curious. The questions show some sort of spiritual activity in their lives. God is at work, and we must take their questions seriously.

- *The Church Attendance Signal:* It is always significant when seekers come to church. When they show up, Christians should assume God is at work in their lives. Going to church is one way seekers attempt to respond to their spiritual confusion.

- *The Christian Literature Signal:* Pay attention when seekers tell you they have started reading the Bible or a religious book. What they read indicates a need in their lives. They are searching and we must try and understand what is prompting the search.

- *The Christian Broadcasting Signal:* When non-Christians mention they listened to a Christian radio program or watched a Christian program on television, ask some followup questions. Find out what they thought about the program. Ask them to tell you about the speaker's message. Monitor their reactions to see how they responded.

- *The Christian Fellowship Signal:* If seekers join with Christians in some sort of fellowship activity, the event has spiritual significance. For some seekers, attending a fellowship activity with a Christian friend is a trial-balloon to help them decide if they will attend a church service later. The seekers will evaluate the Christians in the fellowship setting to see if there is anything distinctive about their lives.

With seekers, the spiritual signals are subtle but clear. As lostologists, we know the importance of these signals and must never take them for granted. Beneath the calm, controlled questions and other subtle signals hides a person seeking God. We, as Christians, must be ready to provide the directions that help seekers take the next step.

THE LOSTOLOGY LAB

Recall a time when you stopped and asked for directions. Now consider these questions:

- If a security video camera filmed you as you asked for directions, what would the tape have revealed? How did you look? How did you sound?

- If you had been hooked up to an Emotion Meter Monitor while you asked for directions and this meter provided a complete printout of what you were thinking and feeling, what would the printout have revealed?

Recall some of the spiritual seekers you have encountered. Think about the ways they signaled to you that they were searching for spiritual answers. Now answer these questions:

- Have you ever missed a spiritual signal from a seeker? What was the signal? Why did you miss it? How did you discover that you had missed the signal?

- Why do you think many Christians in churches fail to catch the significance of questions and other signals seekers give? What can be done to raise the sensitivity of these Christians to the seekers around them?

- Of the spiritual signals listed in this chapter, which ones have you encountered most often as you have interacted with seekers?

- Which of the signals do you consider to be the most significant?

- Which of the signals do you tend to dismiss as less significant?

COMING NEXT: MEASURED WORDS

All right, let's say we tune in and notice a seeker friend who is really pursuing spiritual insights. What do we do then? What do we say? How much do we say? The eleventh law of lostology covered in the next chapter helps us get ready. Without a thorough understanding of this law, our enthusiastic attempt at spiritual directions can cause real problems.

Confusing Directions

The way of peace they do not know;
there is no justice in their paths.
They have turned them into crooked roads . . .

Isaiah 59:8

Lostology Law #11

Directions are always confusing.

Portland, Oregon, is a city laced with meandering rivers. The Columbia, the Willamette, the Clackamas, and the Tualatin rivers wander through the city the way raindrops squiggle down a pane of glass. City planners faced a great challenge when they developed this city among the rivers. The result was a city laced together by a graceful collection of bridges: the Steel bridge, the Markham bridge, the Burnside bridge, the Sellwood bridge, to name only a few.

Local people relate easily to Portland's family of bridges. Like relatives at a reunion, people call the bridges by their first names. When giving directions, they comfortably say, "Go past the Sellwood then stay on 43 and take the Markham." That is fine if you know the bridge family and can name all the sisters. Unfortunately, for an outsider, these directions defy understanding.

Look on a map of Portland and you do not see bridge names. All you find is a street or highway that goes over water. Driving to the bridges won't help. None wear name tags. The stranger on a blind date with

Portland's bridge sisters is doomed to play guessing games all night. Strangers rarely guess correctly.

In the early days of my time in Portland, I often confused my bridges. As I attempted to follow someone's directions, I often found myself in the fast lane to Seattle when I wanted to head toward San Francisco. It wasn't that people tried to confuse me. What they said was accurate. It wasn't that people refused to help me. They did all they could to guide me. They were simply bumping into a basic law of lostology, the eleventh in our study: directions are always confusing.

Well Intentioned but Confusing

Think about the people who have given you directions over the years. Overall, would you say those directions have been crystal clear? No way! They talked. You listened. Then you stared, muddled around, and banged and bumped as you tried to do what they said. Ultimately, you questioned the wisdom and integrity of the person who gave you the directions in the first place. Face it. Most people give crummy directions.

Just Not Helpful

Why do people who want to be helpful inevitably give confusing directions? Here are a few key reasons:

- Direction givers struggle to explain routes they follow automatically. Many cannot name all the streets they follow to a particular location. This leads to statements like: "I know how to get there; I just don't know how to tell you." They have driven the route so often, they do so without thinking. For them, it's auto-drive all the way.

- Direction givers assume you know more than you do. Even if you tell them you have never been in the area before, they will invariably give directions that require a basic understanding of the area. They cannot remember what it is like to know nothing about their town. Try as they might, they simply cannot shift back to a zero-level of knowledge.

- Direction givers talk too fast. The information they give may be accurate, but it cannot be processed. As a result, the directions become mental mush. Lost people, embarrassed to ask for help in the first place, nod and smile even when they are totally confused. As soon as they get back to their cars, they realize they have no idea what they were told.

- What direction givers say is an approximation of reality. If they sketch a map on a napkin, they will draw the streets in straight lines. They will leave out small jogs in the road and ignore cross streets. When they say to turn at the fifth light, they may overlook the blinking yellow light in their count. Lost people, on the other hand, follow directions literally. The gap between the approximate directions and geographic reality may be profound. This gap dooms people to stay lost.

- Direction givers often underestimate the difficulty of getting to a particular destination. When asked for help, they respond, "Sure, that's no problem. All you need to do is . . . " They are correct. It is easy to get there—if you have lived in the town for thirty years. People who are familiar with an area grow comfortable with it and forget how confusing it is to those who see it for the first time. As a result, people give directions that oversimplify the turns and stops that stand between the lost person and the ultimate destination.

In the end, even with their best intentions, people end up frustrating lost people as much as they help. The eleventh law of lostology stands unbroken: directions are always confusing.

WHAT A CONTRAST

The Pharisees were a well-intentioned group—well-intentioned but dead wrong. They majored on giving spiritual directions. No one surpassed them. They mastered the Old Testament law and the writings of others who interpreted the law. Over time, they developed elaborate systems of theology. These complex systems became impossible to follow, even for the Pharisees. Still, they hounded others to embrace their religious system. No wonder the people were confused. No wonder Jesus called the Pharisees "blind guides."

Enter Jesus. From the first, people knew He was different. When Jesus related to spiritual outsiders, He spoke to them in language they understood. He told stories. He wrapped spiritual messages in everyday images.

On one occasion, Jesus used a series of parables about knocking on doors, wide and narrow gates, good trees and bad trees, and wise and foolish builders to communicate spiritual truths. The people listening compared Jesus to the Pharisees in this way:

> When Jesus had finished saying these things, the crowds were amazed at His teaching, because He taught as one who had authority, and not as their teachers of the law. (Matt. 7:28-29)

The Pharisees confused the people. Jesus came as The Way, The Truth, and The Life. As the master Communicator, Jesus wanted His listeners to understand what He taught. Even if they did not grasp the full impact of the truth, they received the seeds of truth. In time, those seeds could germinate understanding in their hearts. They would be confused no longer.

A CLASS FOR SEEKERS

Of the many strategies we tried at our new church to improve communication with secular people, one of the biggest flops was our seeker class on Sunday morning. Good idea; lousy implementation.

We did have a few seekers show up. That was not the problem. Our obstacle was the Christians who wanted to help in the class. Before we began, we explained that our purpose was to encourage a discussion with our seeker friends and respond to their questions and issues. "Great," everyone said. "That's just what we'll do." Unfortunately, that is just what they did *not* do.

In spite of their good intentions, most of our Christian helpers wandered off on two extremes. Some chased their own agendas, raising personal questions that left our seekers perplexed. Others stayed on the subject but couched their comments in Christian jargon and vague scriptural references. Once again, our seekers felt frustrated.

The most positive impact on the group was made by the new Christians who met with us. They could still relate to the seekers and did not use Christian cliches or bring up obscure biblical references. No one could fault our Christians for trying to give helpful spiritual directions. They tried hard. Unfortunately, they added to the fog through which the seekers had to navigate.

BREAKING THE CONFUSION BARRIER

Relating to secular people requires a cultural adaptation for most Christians. We have to think about what we say and strive to find common ground for understanding. This requires hard work and clear thinking. Here are a few steps that can help:

- Don't assume seekers know anything about the Bible or spiritual principles. Even if they have a basic foundation of understanding, it is better to build from the ground up. Don't risk leaving them confused from the outset.

- Don't use religious cliches or obscure theological terms in the discussion. References to redemption, atonement, sanctification, and other theological terms force seekers to guess your meaning. It is fine to talk about any of these biblical concepts or terms. Just be sure and take the time to explain them first.

- Don't cover too much material too quickly. Take your time and build concepts slowly. Secular people need time to assimilate new ideas.

- Don't be concerned if non-Christians ask questions that deal with matters other than the topic at hand. Their questions reveal their concerns and interests. It will be difficult for them to focus on what you want to tell them until their questions are addressed. Respond to what they ask. Listen. Move ahead when they are satisfied with what has been discussed already.

Like Jesus, we must use today's language to communicate the truths of eternity. What a challenge. We need to take unchangeable spiritual truths and couch them in language people understand. Spiritual directions will always be confusing for people—at least at first. If we do our job as communicators, we can minimize the confusion and help our seeker friends take a step toward God.

THE LOSTOLOGY LAB

- Think about the times people have given you directions. Were those directions clear and easy to follow? If not, why not?

- People do not intend to give confusing directions, yet they still do. Why is this?

- What do you think is the most common mistake direction-givers make which causes confusion?

- Think of a time you gave directions that people had difficulty following. Were the directions clear to you when you gave them? Why do you think the lost people thought they were confusing?

Think of a time you tried to talk to a non-Christian about your faith. Try to remember what you said and how the lost person responded. Now answer these questions:

- Did the person find your spiritual directions clear or confusing?

- If your directions were confusing, what could you have done to make them less confusing?

- Based on the insights you have gained through your study of lostology, what will you do in future conversations with spiritual seekers to make your spiritual directions easier to understand and follow?

COMING NEXT: ENOUGH IS ENOUGH

Not only do Christians often say the wrong things to secular people, we tend to say far more than necessary. Part of the secret of relating to seekers is to know when we have said enough. We will focus on that delicate balance next.

Just the Directions, Please!

Furthermore, tell the people, "This is what the
Lord says: See, I am setting before you the
way of life and the way of death."
Jeremiah 21:8

Lostology Law #12
Unnecessary details make directions more confusing.

My father is to directions what Mozart is to music, what Rembrandt is to painting, and what Shakespeare is to literature. Trips with our family were always well-crafted works of art. Routes were plotted carefully on multiple maps, prime routes highlighted with potential side trip opportunities carefully noted. Questions about any stretch of road invoked lengthy recitations about the mileage, the elevation, and the distance between rest stops.

To these basic directional skills, my dad added AAA—Automobile Association of America—the essential resource for the serious car traveler. As a member he received books with hotel ratings, trip guides, and pamphlets about not-to-be-missed historical markers and scenic over-looks. Planning became a full-time job before, during, and after the trip. Ask my dad about any place in America and he can go to his files and pull out the appropriate books, charts, and records of past trips.

My dad recently added another resource to his formidable directional database: the computerized mapping program. Through the wonders of computer technology, he can now prepare personalized maps for any trip, charted according to driving speed, eating habits, and bladder control.

Although my dad is a gracious, helpful, thorough direction giver, there are times when he slips slightly over the edge. If I call, asking for directions to a particular destination, a few days later a bulky parcel arrives in the mail. The package bulges with a personalized and multi-color highlighted map, old copies of the appropriate AAA guides for each state along the route, plus a written explanation about points of interest.

The ultimate challenge for my dad was the trip I made with my wife and daughters from Portland, Oregon, to Nashville, Tennessee. All his skills converged in a magnificent symphony of directions for that cross-country trip. Never in the history of direction-giving has any family been given such exhaustive, detailed, well-intentioned directions for extended travel. It was directional Mecca, the summit, the high point, the apex. Sort of confusing, but memorable.

A BIT TOO HELPFUL

Have you ever encountered an overly eager direction giver? You know you have one when they light up as soon as you ask for help:

- "I know right where that is, honey. Come round here. I'll just draw you a little map. How long are you going to be staying there? There's lots to see. I have some postcards from our last trip. Isn't that spectacular? Let me tell you about that one. That was the summer . . ."

- "I can get you there the quick way or the pretty way. The quick way's no good cause you've got to go through Delightsville and it's almost lunch time and you'll get caught in the traffic round the Dairy Bar and that'll take you too long. You might as well go the pretty way. All you have to do is go northwest on the farm to market road 1932 and stay on it until you come to the bridge. At the bridge, go right and you'll wind along the ridge above town and it's real pretty. Of course, you could go round north of town on the quick way and miss some of that traffic, but you don't get to see as much. If I was you, I'd . . ."

- "No problem getting there from here. It's 87 miles. As long as you're going that way, you'll want to stop and see the historical marker right outside of town. Tells the history of the boll weevil infestation back in 1926. Six and a half miles past that, there's a pretty nice rest stop. Some folks have their family reunions out there so it may be crowded. You'd better stop when you see it cause it's your last chance to go to the bathroom for an hour or so. After the rest stop, get back on the main road and follow it through . . . "

Nice people. Accurate directions. Helpful bits of information. But you are in an awkward position. You need the directions . . . but only to a point! Just another example of Lostology Law #12: Detailed directions add confusion. People don't know when enough is enough.

The Right Dose of Truth

When Jesus interacted with people, He carefully controlled the volume of truth He shared. He knew all truth; He was The Truth. Yet for those seeking spiritual answers, Jesus measured out the truth in portions that matched the individual's capacity to receive.

The disciples constantly badgered Jesus to tell them about topics of interest. Often, Jesus answered their questions directly:

- When they asked Jesus how to pray, he taught them the model prayer (Luke 11:2-4).

- When they asked why they could not heal a sick boy, Jesus rebuked them for their lack of faith (Matt. 17:14-21).

- When they asked who would be greatest in the kingdom of heaven, Jesus explained that unless they changed and became like little children, they would never see the kingdom of heaven(Matt. 18:4).

Other times, Jesus responded to their questions with parables:

- When they asked how many times they should forgive one who sinned against them, Jesus told them a parable about an unmerciful servant (Matt. 18:21-35).

- To teach the disciples about the Kingdom of God, Jesus told them parables about mustard seeds and yeast in dough(Luke 13:18-20).

- To prepare them to sow and reap a spiritual harvest, Jesus told them a parable about a sower who planted seeds in four types of soil with four different results (Luke 8:4-15).

Yet, on another occasion, Jesus simply told them they were not ready for all he could tell them. They would have to wait. Jesus said:

I have much more to say to you, more than you can now bear. (John 16:12)

What sensitivity! Jesus did not tell them all He knew. He did not even tell them all they wanted to know. He told them exactly what they needed to know. He never dumptrucked truth all over people. He watched. He waited. When the time was right, He gave them more.

DUMPTRUCK EVANGELISM

One of the hardest disciplines for me in relating to secular people is knowing when to stop talking. My greatest struggle occurs when I meet intellectual seekers who ask provocative questions. Inevitably, I battle the temptation to tell them far more than they need to hear.

Marsha was a thoughtful, intellectual seeker. She visited our church along with her two children. She was analytical, articulate, and skeptical. As I preached, all I saw was the top of her head, never her face. Initially, I thought she was bored or reading something in her lap. Later, I discovered she was taking extensive notes. As she listened, she wrote comments, questions, and her evaluation of what I said.

After the services, I looked forward to talking with Marsha. She asked challenging questions. As a systematic thinker, she struggled to place her newly acquired knowledge about Christianity into tidy intellectual boxes. She explained her ideas to me and summarized her understanding of what I said, then proclaimed how she reconciled her ideas with my ideas. It was fascinating—totally off-the-wall, but fascinating.

Marsha oversimplified the truths we were discussing. Other concepts, she misunderstood all together. I tried to broaden her thinking, to stretch her, to challenge her. To a degree, I did. Yet, I discovered that if I pushed too far, she resisted and began to pull back. There was so much I wanted to tell her, but for the moment, she had all she could handle. She quickly reached her capacity to process new information. More information at that point would have been counterproductive.

TELLING THE TRUTH WITH WISDOM

When talking with inquisitive seekers, I still get excited. I still talk more than I should and listen less than I could. On occasion, I even raise questions seekers are not asking. I am learning to control that impulse. James 1:19 provides a guideline I try to follow: "Everyone should be quick to listen, slow to speak, and slow to become angry . . ."

We want to say everything we can think of when we have the opportunity to talk about spiritual things. In our zeal to share the gospel, we can bury seekers with too much information. Our noble attempts at spiritual directions can ultimately confuse rather than help.

Many of the best evangelistic training programs today center on extensive, memorized gospel presentations. These programs are excellent and prepare Christians to explain the essential truths of our faith. However, we must practice discernment while sharing the information we have learned.

When Christians share lengthy, memorized gospel overviews during initial encounters with a lost person, I sometimes cringe. In their desire to present the gospel, these Christians discourage the questions the seeker wants to ask. They lock the person into an extended listening mode suggesting that questions can be asked later. I have watched listener's body language during these extended monologues. They appeared confused, even irritated. But the monologue went on and on.

Comprehensive gospel presentations can be helpful when someone is ready hear the full scope of the gospel plan. There is a time to dump your truck, to tell someone all you know, and to answer every question.

However, with seekers in the early stages of their searches, it is often more effective to share information bit by bit in response to specific questions. Each encounter should be tailored to the needs of the lost person. Answers to questions people ask are always more readily received than information presented to them like a sales pitch.

SMALL DOSES OF THE TRUTH

One of the benefits of memorizing a comprehensive presentation of the gospel is knowing you can adapt the information to fit each witnessing situation. If you learn the plan of salvation taught in Continuing Witness Training[4] or Evangelism Explosion[5], you can use sections of the presentation, individual Scriptures, and even illustrations to respond to the needs and interests of the person with whom you are sharing. Here are a few practical guidelines:

- Listen as much as you talk. By listening, you earn the right to talk. By understanding, you earn the right to be understood.

- Ask questions to insure you are being understood. Do not talk for an extended period of time without stopping to see if your friend has questions. Once people get confused at one point, that confusion compounds as more information is shared. Move slowly and check for understanding often. Simply ask, "Does this make sense to you?" People will tell you!

- Use parts of your memorized presentation to respond to specific questions your seeker friend asks. Communicating the truth in smaller doses enhances understanding. In the end, you will have the chance to share all you need to say about the gospel. You will simply allow time for discussion and questions as you go.

- Avoid sharing your ideas in a manner that sounds like a canned "sales pitch." Most people enjoy talking with people. Few of us enjoy talking with salesmen. Use what you know about the gospel to simply talk about the gospel. Explain in a natural way how your non-Christian friend can have a relationship with Christ.

Most Christians want to share the gospel with lost people. We long to give spiritual directions. We simply need God's wisdom to know how much to say. Like Jesus, we must be able to say: "I have more to tell you, but you can't handle it all right now." If we are sensitive to God's leadership and sensitive to the lost people we talk with, God will help us share the truth in the proper doses.

THE LOSTOLOGY LAB

- Have you ever encountered an overly eager direction-giver? Describe the person. What did he or she say and do?

- Describe your optimum type of directions, those which contain the perfect balance of broad information and specific details.

- When you ask for directions, how often do you get this perfect balance?

- When you talk with non-Christians about Christ, do you tend to say too much or too little? Why?

- Describe a time in witnessing when you said too much. What did the person do to let you know you had given confusing directions?

- Have you used a memorized gospel presentation to share your faith with non-Christians? How effective has this strategy been for you?

- How do you feel about the idea of adapting a memorized presentation in response to the questions and concerns expressed by the non-Christian with whom you are talking?

- What changes will you make in the future as you interact with secular people to make sure the spiritual directions you give are helpful rather than confusing?

Coming Next: Shifting into Search Mode

It is one thing to get lost. Few people have been hurt by getting lost on a trip or on their way to an appointment. It is irritating, sometimes humorous, but not dangerous. Not so when a person is missing. The danger is real. The lessons change. The skills change. The sense of urgency grows. It is time to shift into search mode.

PART THREE

The Cost of Being Lost

Misplaced Valuables

You have not strengthened the weak
or healed the sick or bound up the injured.
You have not brought back the strays
or searched for the lost.
Ezekiel 34:4

Lostology Law #13
A search reveals your values.

A search always reveals your values. My values changed on March 1, 1980. On that day, my bride, Lynn Marie, placed a gold ring on my finger. And from that day on I lived in fear—not of my wife, but fear of when I would lose my wedding ring.

Notice I said *when* not *if*. Keeping up with small objects has never been easy for me. Marriage did not alter that character flaw. Over the years, I have lost, searched for, and found my wedding ring numerous times. Unfortunately, the frequency with which I lost my ring increased over time. 1990 was a bad year.

First I lost my ring at the health club. Family friction mounted, then eased when a club staff member found the ring among the dirty towels. Later that year, I lost my ring again. This time, I was clueless about its location. Lynn Marie always took it hard when I lost my wedding ring, so I usually searched incognito for as long as possible. I finally got desperate and half-jokingly asked a lady at our church to pray I would find my ring. A strange thing happened. The next day, Lynn Marie walked up and asked,

"Did you leave your ring in the guest room?" I took the ring. "Guess I did," I replied, and placed it on my finger. *Squeaked through another scare,* I told myself.

Perhaps God felt I had congratulated myself too much on that search and rescue operation. Soon I faced the climactic challenge, the big one, the mother of all ring losses.

During a water balloon fight with the kids from our church in a local park, I lobbed my wedding ring along with a water-swollen balloon toward an unsuspecting kid. Instant trouble. Only I didn't know the ring was missing until I arrived back at my office. By then, the chances of finding that ring were approximately the same as being able to glue together all the busted balloons scattered across that park.

Driven by the twin emotions of dread and resolve, I began my search. "What are you looking for?" people asked. "My wedding ring," I replied, hoping they had picked it up. "Oh, that's too bad," the women said, with pained expressions on their faces. Not so with the men. They gave me knowing nods that said, "Your fat's in the fire now, buddy." They were right.

I never found that ring. Not because I didn't look, you understand. Faithfully, earnestly, devotedly, I scoured the ground, scuffing around, picking through branches, and shifting through piles of debris. In the history of mankind and wedding rings, no one has ever demonstrated greater commitment to a matrimonial symbol. I valued that ring. No one doubted that . . . not even my wife.

But the grim reality settled upon me: that ring was history. Defeated, I broke the news to Lynn Marie. She said she was crushed. But she knew how to deal with our loss. New, matching wedding rings—that would dull the pain, she said. Caught without recourse, I conceded. Off we trooped, checkbook in hand, new rings in our hearts.

I searched for my old ring because I valued that ring. When I lose my new ring (note the *when* . . . not *if*), I will search for it also. A search always reveals our values.

Value Judgments

Recall two things you have lost—one you searched for and one you didn't. Let's start with the item you lost then searched for. Got it in mind? Consider these questions:

- Why did you search for it?

- How long did you search?

- If your search was successful, how did you feel?

- If your search was unsuccessful, how did you feel?

Now think about the item you lost but did not search for. Got it? Ask yourself these questions:

- Why didn't you search?

- How did you feel about losing the item?

- What did you do to compensate for the loss?

We rarely stop and think about our decisions to search for lost items. Instinctively, we make decisions to search or not search based on personal criteria. We gain insight if we reflect on the decisions we make:

- We search for what we value. If we lose something and choose not to search for it, we essentially say we place little value on that item. Actions, not words, reveal our values.

- Losing items of minimal value is an inconvenience. Losing something of great value can be a tragedy.

- Disposable items can always be replaced. However, some lost valuables create a void no substitute can fill.

- The more we value something that is lost, the longer we search for it. For items of minimal value, we search for a few minutes. For items of high value, we search for hours. For items of infinite value, we search indefinitely.

If we switch our focus from lost things to lost people, the issues change dramatically. Lostology helps us make this shift. If a search always reveals our values, what does a lack of evangelism reveal? As lostologists, we know the answer. No search . . . no value.

THE HIGHEST VALUE

Throughout Jesus' earthly ministry, people tried to write mission statements for Him:

- The excitable crowd urged Jesus to be their political messiah, the long-awaited one who would lead the Jews to throw off Rome's military domination.

- The religious types expected Jesus to be a good rabbi, to teach the people without stirring up trouble or challenging the religious assumptions of the day.

- Home town acquaintances expected Jesus to blend into community life—working as the son of the carpenter, another sibling among sisters and brothers, a good son who would care for his mother.

Jesus resisted all who tried to set His mission for Him. He knew why He had come. Jesus explained His mission succinctly in Luke 19:10: "For the Son of Man came to seek and save what was lost."

Jesus' mission on earth centered on searching for lost people. Why? Values. Jesus' mission grew out of God's value system. In Matthew 18:14, Jesus affirmed the value His heavenly Father placed on people: "In the same way your Father in heaven is not willing that any of these little ones should be lost."

Driven by his heavenly Father's value system, Jesus centered His earthly ministry on lost people:

- Jesus personally searched for lost people. Lost people sensed His love. Jesus invested much of His time interacting with lost people, explaining spiritual truths to them, and helping them find the relationship with God for which they longed.

- Jesus trained a spiritual search and rescue force. For over three years, He equipped his disciples with the values and skills to minister to lost people. His final commission to them was to launch a worldwide mission to find the lost.

- Jesus empowered His disciples so they could multiply His search and rescue team. The book of Acts and Christian history reveal the impact of His strategy and the effectiveness of those mobilized to share the good news.

- Jesus offered hope to all who seek God. He died on the cross and rose from the dead to pay the sin-debt that separates lost people from God. He paid every account in full. He built the bridge for lost people to travel on their way home to God.

If a search reveals values, Jesus' values blazed bright. People mattered to him. As a result He searched for them . . . for us. Why? Because God values us; God loves us.

The apostle John captured the emotional impact of this search when he wrote in John 3:16, "For God so loved the world that He gave His one and only son, that whoever believes in Him shall not perish but have eternal life." No greater statement of value has ever been made. This objective standard of value is the measure against which we must evaluate our actions as Christians.

FEEBLE EXCUSES

In spite of God's love for people and His assessment of value for each of us, Christians still struggle with evangelism. As a Christian insider, I have struggled as much as anyone. Along the way, many of us have rationalized why we don't share our faith more often or more effectively. Have you heard (or even used) any of these?

- Evangelism is not my gift. Since it's not my gift, people shouldn't pressure me to share my faith. I need to discover my gifts and use them in my ministry. Until then, leave me alone.

- I don't have time. With my involvement in church and ministry, I'm simply too busy to develop relationships with lost people. Sure, I could make time for that, but think of all the good things I'd have to stop doing.

- I don't know any non-Christians. Since I became a Christian, I'm just not comfortable around secular people. Inevitably, they do things and say things that have a negative impact on those around them, including me. Hasn't God called us to be separate and holy people?

- I need more training. I need to learn more about evangelism before I do evangelism. But don't suggest Continuing Witness Training, Evangelism Explosion, or any other course which includes actual experiences in witnessing. I prefer to learn about evangelism in ways that don't involve talking with lost people.

No matter how we shine up these rationalizations, they dull in light of God's value system. If God loved us enough to launch the ultimate spiritual search for us, what should we do with the lost people around us?

Obviously, we should tell them about the God who loves them. Failure to go and tell reveals a sick value system that needs a transfusion of God's love.

FACING THE TRUTH

How ironic that most Christians struggle so much with evangelism. Ask us why and we may claim we don't know what to say. Press us and we may say we feel uncomfortable talking with non-Christians. Push further and we may admit we are afraid our efforts to share our faith could do more harm than good.

Yet the deeper truth may be darker. If a search reveals values, a decision not to search also reveals values. Perhaps we don't seek to share our faith more because people are not really valuable to us. If so, we must confront the fact that people do not matter to us as much as they matter to God.

Facing this uncomfortable truth may be the first step in adjusting our thinking, our living, and our values. In reality, we probably do not need more training in evangelism. We simply need new hearts . . . and more love.

If we valued people as God values people, we would live differently. As lostologists, let's be honest enough to drop the rationalizations and confront the real issues. Any search or no search always reveals our values.

THE LOSTOLOGY LAB

- When you lose an item, how do you decide if you will search for it or not? How do you decide how long you will search?

- How are your personal values revealed in the type of search you launch for items you lose?

- How did Jesus reveal the value He placed on lost people by the way He lived His life on earth?

- What value do you place on lost people? How do your actions reveal your values?

- Do you find that what you do in evangelism is sometimes inconsistent with the value you claim to place on lost people? How do you deal with this inconsistency?

- What reasons or rationalizations do you use with yourself or with others to explain why you do not devote more time to sharing your faith with lost people?

- Do you find it is easier to talk about evangelism, and learn about evangelism, than to actually do evangelism? If so, how have you seen this in your life?

- How well do your values about lost people line up with God's values about lost people? Do you want God to change your values?

- If God changed your value system regarding lost people, how would that change the way you live on a daily basis?

COMING NEXT: SEARCHING FOR THE RIGHT PRICE

We live in a world of discounts. Can we ever expect a spiritual search to be anything less than costly? Our next study tackles this issue.

The Discount Search Store

The kingdom of heaven is like treasure hidden in a field.
When a man found it, he hid it again,
and then in his joy went and sold all
he had and bought that field.
Matthew 13:44

Lostology Law #14
Searches are always costly.

Flip open your Yellow Pages. Check under "search and rescue." Find any discount search companies? Check carefully for any of these advertisements:

- Honest Herb's Handy Searches. You lose them; we find them. Best prices in town. Your hometown search store.

- Lotty's Cut-Rate Lost and Found. 17 years experience. Custom searches by caring professionals. You can't find what you lost for less!

- SearchFax. Don't let a search interrupt your busy schedule. Leave the searching to us. Fax the information. We'll keep you posted. All major credit cards accepted.

- Wee-Search-R-Us. We do the small searches others turn down. See our coupon on page 231. Half-price searches every Friday.

- Sniff-n-Scent, Inc. Trained search chihuahuas. Top searches in tight places. Rent our dogs by the hour or by the day. Easy pick up and drop off. All dogs house broken.

- Zelma's Hide And Seek. Zelma Ezell, owner. 31 years of money-saving searches and satisfied customers. You don't pay extra for our experience.

- LostLine International. Call 1-900-SOO-LOST. Why pay for high-priced searchers when our trained professionals can help you organize your own search? $2.73 per minute. Hundreds less than you'd spend on a traditional search. For updates on our worldwide search for Elvis, ask for operator 146.

What did you find in your local Yellow Pages? You're right—there are no discount search and rescue organizations. Why? Because searches require time and money and lots of both. Lostology Law #13 drives home this truth: searches are always costly.

CLARIFYING THE ISSUE

We watch with horror when news stories tell of missing children. As parents, we shiver as we personalize the tragedy unfolding for another family. While we listen, we wonder how we would respond. What would we do?

One thing we know for sure: if someone in our family were missing, we would pay whatever was required. At that point, money would not be the concern. What we needed, we would get. Time would not be an issue either. We would spend the time necessary to complete the search. Our only focus would be finding the one who was lost.

Although few of us have ever faced a search situation personally, we know intuitively that a search is inherently costly. Time and money? We expect a search to require both.

Only in spiritual search and rescue do we alter these expectations. *We want evangelism that does not demand time and church outreach that does not cost money.* Such expectations are unrealistic and contrary to everything we know about search efforts. How unfortunate that our thinking becomes fuzzy at this point, especially in light of God's clear affirmation of the cost of a spiritual search.

A High Price Paid

The Bible, from beginning to end, proclaims the incredible price God was willing to pay for a lost world. Stained in blood, the cross stands as the ultimate price tag for a search and rescue operation. In eternity and throughout history, God determined to pay the price required for our salvation:

- Before time began, God anticipated sin and the sacrifice required. Christ, the Lamb of God, was slain before the foundation of the world in the heart of God.

- Before He created the world, God knew the full reality of sin and the necessity of a savior.

- Before He created the first human being, God knew that mankind would be a prodigal and need a loving Father to call him home.

- Before God entered into a covenant relationship with a nation of people, He knew people would prostitute their love and need a Redeemer to buy them back from disgrace.

- Before God began to call people to an eternal banquet table, He knew most would reject the invitation and would need a persistent host to call until all who declined were without excuse.

- Before God began a ministry on earth proclaiming love's good news, He knew people would reject the gospel and crucify love.

God chose to pay the ultimate price for us. In the cross, God proved the truth that a search is always costly. To think otherwise, we must ignore Calvary.

A New Church's Price Tag

The Westside Baptist Church in Lake Oswego, Oregon, was begun by a massive volunteer effort. Over five hundred families in the First Baptist Church of Garland, Texas, joined other Christians in the northwest to make over forty-seven thousand phone calls into the target area for the new church.

The Texas volunteers alone logged thousands of hours and paid from fifteen to thirty dollars in personal long distance phone bills. The cost of the calls was over twelve thousand dollars. That price does not include thousands of dollars spent mailing brochures to those who requested information about the new church.

The project was an amazing investment of time and money in a spiritual search and rescue activity. Preparation required more than a year. Volunteers worked diligently in the months before the church began.

On March 13, 1988, in the Lake Oswego High School auditorium, 209 people showed up for the first service. About 160 of those attending were true prospects for the new church. Looking over the crowd that morning, I was thankful each person was there. But I also thought about the thousands we called who did not come. Was it worth all the time? Was the project worth the money we invested? Was it appropriate to spend so much to reach so few?

At the time, I had not discovered the laws of lostology. If I had already known these principles, I would have been ready to answer the "Was it worth it?" question. Time and money have nothing to do with the validity of a search and rescue operation. We do not search because it is convenient or cost effective. We do not evaluate a search on a ratio of "lost found" to "resources invested." Love compels us to search. We expect a search to be costly so we are not surprised when it is.

The Practical Price Tag

Evangelism will never be easy or inexpensive for a church or for an individual. Reaching out and searching for lost people demands time and money. There is no alternative.

- Evangelism will impact our planning calendars. Reaching lost people for Christ will take time. Building relationships with non-Christians will mean we cannot do other things we want to do—good things, things we would enjoy doing. Relationships do not develop automatically. They require time and emotional energy. Since the most effective evangelism is relational, time for nurturing relationships is essential.

- Evangelism will impact our checkbooks. Thousands of new churches are needed in America to reach lost people who cannot be reached by existing churches. Existing churches must channel funds into innovative outreach programs to reach lost people in their communities and invest funds to begin new churches. Mission organizations need millions of dollars to launch international search operations.

Who will give this money? Christians, of course. We must give! We who have found our way to the cross must sacrifice so others can find their way. It will cost more than ever before. We must be willing to pay the price.

Evangelism requires sacrifice. Money? Yes. Time? Of course. Evangelism will cost us. It was expensive to find us when we were lost. Others paid that bill. Now it is our turn.

Ultimately, any discussion of sacrifice must measure our investment against the standard of the cross. Only as we look at the cross do the issues shift into focus. Only the cross insures that love will keep us searching for the lost.

THE LOSTOLOGY LAB

- If you needed to launch a search, how expensive do you think that search would be? You would expect to get help from the police, but what if they could not do all you thought needed to be done? Who else would you call? How much money would you expect to spend?

- How would you respond to a person who was attempting to launch a search for a missing person, but who constantly complained about how much the search was costing and how much time it was requiring? How would you feel about that person?

- In what ways is evangelism costly in terms of time? In what ways are evangelism and church outreach costly in terms of money?

- In what ways do we, as Christians, give the impression that we expect evangelism and church outreach to be convenient and inexpensive?

- We know what God paid to offer salvation to us. How do we reconcile what He did for us when we were lost with what we are willing to do to reach the lost around us?

- You have thought about the inherent cost of a spiritual search. What practical changes do you need to make in the way you spend your time and money so you can be involved in evangelism and church outreach?

COMING NEXT: THE EFFECTIVE SEARCH

At some point, we must account for the cost of a search and the results achieved. The bottom-line we reach and the evaluation we make will be determined by the accounting system we use. We will evaluate two systems in our next study.

Heart Accounting

And I pray that you . . . may grasp
how wide and long and high and deep
is the love of Christ,
and to know this love that surpasses knowledge.
Ephesians 3:17-19

Lostology Law #15
Love pays whatever the search costs.

The potluck stands central in church life today. Denominations may argue about an array of doctrinal concerns, but we stand in amazing unity on the issue of potlucks. Potlucks are good.

The problem is, potlucks are boring. Face it. There is a limit to how creative you can be with a potluck. The goals are too simplistic: assemble the maximum amount of food, eat the maximum amount of food, leave the maximum amount of food behind for the hostess.

Creative churchgoers at some point in Christian history developed a variation of the potluck called the progressive potluck. All basic goals of the traditional potluck remain intact. Only now, it is possible to eat even more because short periods of digestion are imposed as the potluckers troop from house to house.

Progressive potlucks can be dangerous. Few rules are written and most groups learn what does and does not work through trial and error. One foundational rule stands tested through the centuries: preschoolers should never be part of a progressive potluck. One small group in our church dared to defy this ancient guideline.

ACT ONE

These young adults had an odd gene assortment that predetermined their children would be less than five years old and female. My wife and I, along with our two daughters, joined the group in a fool's adventure: progressive potluck *a la* preschoolers. By stop number two, the folly of our choice was evident.

In a desperate bid to buy time, three of us volunteered to take the group of nine little girls for a walk. Our logic was adequate: herd them around the block, use up energy, then stall for time until the next home. Out the door we headed, herding the preschool girls like a parade of crickets. Three adults, nine preschoolers. You'd think that was an adequate ratio. Wrong!

The preschoolers, sensing an opportunity, immediately used the old "divide and conquer" strategy. All ran and scattered:

- One girl, the youngest, immediately tripped, crashed, and burned. First aid pulled one adult off the pursuit.

- Three preschoolers thundered down the sidewalk, a long steady hill that accelerated their speed until their chubby legs blurred with motion. Their exodus and the corresponding chase occupied another adult.

- Three of the girls followed the others down the hill but slowly fell behind then veered toward the street. I focused on them, yelling for them to get back on the sidewalk while doing my best to shield them from oncoming traffic.

- The remaining girls orbited among the other groups according to a mystic social gravitational pull or until they ventured within grabbing distance of one of the adults.

As responsible adults, we quickly realized we were out of control. Calmly, we faced the facts. There was little chance we were going to return with all nine girls.

ACT TWO

Stop the scene. For the sake of the story, let's say we returned with only seven girls. Surely a 77.7 percent return should be acceptable considering the challenge we faced. We could have calmly explained to the parents what had happened, pointing out the fact that although we were not sure where two of their daughters were, we were confident they had ended up somewhere in the neighborhood.

So as not to hinder the ongoing progression of the potluck, we could have suggested that we focus on the seven girls we had in hand rather than placing inappropriate emphasis on the two preschoolers who were missing. The neighborhood was good. Chances of the girls ending up with a good family were way above average.

Absurd? Certainly. When it comes to lost children, logic ends. Forget calculations. Drop the concept of "acceptable losses." With missing children, we do not add on our fingers; we add in our hearts.

TOUCHING YOUR HEART

Most evenings I hate to watch the news. The relentless parade of tragedy numbs the senses. How do you respond to the stories? To the pictures?

- accounts of children killed or hurt

- stories about babies who are sick or malnourished

- pictures of teenagers who are homeless or abused

Standing in the icy flood of information, do you sense yourself slipping into emotional deadness? Do you begin to listen to facts without seeing real faces? It is easy to do, even understandable. Easy, but not right.

We know intellectually that the children in those stories are real people. The statistics cited refer to someone's children . . . just like our own, like our nieces, nephews or grandchildren. Of course, if those reports referred to our families, we would view the broadcast differently—the report would crush our hearts.

When it comes to people, we cannot view losses objectively, dispassionately, like a cost accountant studying a balance sheet. With people, we choose instead to assess every loss and evaluate appropriate responses through an accounting of the heart. Our hearts lead us to Lostology Law #15. We search because our hearts leave us no option.

Unacceptable Loss

Let's focus again on Jesus' story about the shepherd who had one hundred sheep. One evening, upon counting his flock, he discovered that he had ninety-nine sheep in the fold and one sheep missing in the field. As a good shepherd, he left the ninety-nine who were found to search for the one that was lost.

From a business standpoint, such a move was ludicrous. Imagine an accountant's response upon hearing about the shepherd's decision:

"I can't believe you did that!" the accountant would say. "Forget the one. Focus on the ninety-nine. One missing sheep is an acceptable loss. Write it off on your taxes. That's just the price of doing business."

Such a view is appropriate if you view life from the bottom-line up. But the shepherd worked from a different perspective. His actions sprang from an accounting of the heart. No matter how many sheep were in the fold, he could not rest as long as one was missing. One missing sheep was an unacceptable loss in his heart.

How fortunate for us that our heavenly Father has the heart of the shepherd and not the heart of the cost accountant. In 2 Peter 3:9, the apostle Peter wrote:

The Lord is not slow in keeping his promise, as some understand slowness. He is patient with you, not wanting anyone to perish, but everyone to come to repentance.

God could have easily considered any of us as an acceptable loss. But He didn't. He couldn't. His heart called for a different view of the bottom line.

Evaluating the Bottom Line

During the weeks that followed the first service of our new church in Portland, I got to know the people who came as a result of our outreach project. As we got acquainted, they shared their stories. Most came as a result of some sort of need in their lives. They needed something and were looking for answers. They brought their fears, but carried hope as well.

Initially, none of them knew about the search and rescue operation launched on their behalf. They did not know how many people had worked and sacrificed or how much money had been spent to reach them. Was it worth it?

A cost accountant would have given an answer easily. He would have worked out the averages and determined the cost per attender ratio for our new church. The cost ratio was staggering. As an objective evaluator, the cost accountant could have easily said, "This project wasn't worth the cost."

If you talked to the people who found our church and who ultimately found Christ, they would have given a different answer. Was it worth it? To them, yes, without question. Their evaluation would have been based on an accounting of the heart.

What assessment would you make? The answer you give depends on the accounting system you use.

Good Stewardship of the Heart

In churches today there is a need for financial accountability, for good stewardship. Limited resources cannot, however, become the primary reason for cutting back the search activities of the church.

Looking only at the budget, we will never find a good time to launch a search effort. It will always be too expensive; the results will always be too small. If we are not careful, we can slip into a cost accounting mode and focus on the ninety-nine in the fold rather than the one that is lost. Of course, in most churches today, the numbers are opposite—it's the one in the fold and the ninety-nine who are lost. It is imperative that we make the right choice as we contemplate a search.

Tough-Minded Love

Making wise choices about the use of resources will always be a struggle. There are always more good things that need to be done than we can do. Shortly before His crucifixion, Jesus' disciples questioned Him for allowing a woman to anoint His head with expensive perfume. "This perfume could have been sold for a high price," they said, "and the money given to the poor." In Matthew 26:10-13, Jesus stunned His disciples with His response:

> Why are you bothering this woman? She has done a beautiful thing to me. The poor you will always have with you, but you will not always have me. When she poured this perfume on my body, she did it to prepare me for burial. I tell you the truth, wherever this gospel is preached throughout the world, what she has done will also be told, in memory of her.

Was Jesus demeaning the value of helping the poor? Of course not. He was preparing His disciples to make tough stewardship decisions that defied simplistic solutions. Priorities compete with one another, especially when those priorities call for financial resources. The decisions hinge on alternatives. Jesus affirmed the woman's choice to anoint Him rather than help the poor. He made the tough call about what was most important at that time. Jesus' disciples disagreed with Him. So it will be as we struggle to make decisions in the face of profound spiritual needs. Here are some criteria to consider as we seek God's direction in how we use the resources He has entrusted to us:

- *Window of Opportunity:* We may have a unique opportunity to reach the lost now that may not be ours in the future.

- *Immediate Accountability:* We should determine how the proposed expenditure for evangelism compares to the funds we are already spending on those who are in the church. It is easy to indulge ourselves while ignoring the lost.

- *Spiritual Values:* Our decision about the proposed expenditure will say something about our values as individuals and as a church. We must determine if our values toward reaching the lost are consistent with those Jesus demonstrated.

- *Ultimate Accountability:* If we choose not to spend funds on outreach, we will use those funds in other ways. No matter what we decide, we must be prepared to account to God for how we invested the resources He entrusted to us.

Even with a commitment to heart-accounting, our decisions will never be easy. God's standard of accounting must be our starting point. We must embrace the struggle love creates in our hearts. Driven by love and seeking only to please God, we know God will give us wisdom when decisions must be made. Above all else, we must be willing to pay whatever a search costs.

THE LOSTOLOGY LAB

- If you had been with the shepherd the night he left the ninety-nine in the fold to look for one lost sheep in the field, what would you have told him? Would you have affirmed his decision? Why or why not?

- The term *acceptable loss* is used to refer to a level of loss that is appropriate or unavoidable in a particular endeavor. The shepherd in Jesus' story could have decided to count the one missing sheep as an acceptable loss and stayed with the ninety-nine. If that was the story, what would the message of such a parable be? What would be the implication of that parable for evangelism?

- In what ways do churches and individuals live as if Jesus' parable told of a shepherd who did not worry about the one missing sheep and who chose to stay with the ninety-nine sheep in the fold?

- 2 Peter 3:9 says God does not want *anyone* to perish but everyone to come to repentance. How does this standard impact our tendency to become dispassionate about the masses of people around us who are spiritually lost?

- In your church, which system of accounting (cost-accounting or heart-accounting) drives the decisions made about evangelism and outreach? What statements and decisions reveal the accounting system being used?

- In your personal life, what system of accounting drives the decisions you make about the money you give to support evangelism and missions in your church? What statements or decisions do you make that reveal the accounting system you use?

Coming Next: All the Way to the Top

Even if our hearts tell us to search, other priorities attempt to elbow their way to the top of our list of activities. Only as clear thinking lostologists can we keep our priorities straight. Our priorities flow from a basic law of lostology—the topic of our next study.

SIXTEEN

Top of the List

You will seek me and find me
when you seek me with all your heart.
Jeremiah 29:13

Lostology Law #16
A search becomes your consuming priority.

My childhood memories are checkered with images of intense searches for prodigal pets. Like most kids, we spanned the gamut of pet categories. Frankly, most were great disappointments.

FISH CATEGORY

Our goldfish tried to squeeze through the tiny passageway in his fishbowl castle—that ceramic decoration that was standard equipment in any fashionable fishbowl. Problem was, our castle passage was too snug for our fish. The fish got stuck and drowned . . . or whatever you call it when a fish can't breath and ends up floating upside down.

RODENT CATEGORY

Hamsters, gerbils—we had them all. The hamsters were the biggest disappointment. While in elementary school, I wanted to raise hamsters so I bought two. For some reason, the female grew twice the size of the male. Although small, the male was very affectionate and willing to help me produce baby hamsters. The female? Not interested. She was a fighter, not a lover. Family dysfunction continued. Then it happened. One morning I checked on my hamsters and was greeted by a gruesome scene. My lady hamster had apparently had all she could take of her persistent, amorous partner. So she killed him . . . and ate half of the remains.

Reptile Category

Our classic pet turtle prompted one of the memorable events on Ridgedale Street. He was an average, unassuming turtle. One of those small, half-dollar sized, moss-green turtles that lived in a kidney-shaped bowl with a plastic palm tree poking out of the center sunning island. We really liked that turtle and fed him flies, bugs, and grass. Most of all, we liked to play with him by putting him on the floor and watching him lumber off at turtle warp speed.

In the midst of playing with him on the floor one day, we got distracted. My mom walked up and asked, "Where's the turtle?" We were clueless. Other priorities had captured our attention. So my mom injected a strong dose of authority and upended our To-Do lists. "Find the turtle . . . now!" It was a mom ultimatum.

Her mandate launched The Raiders of the Lost Turtle. We recruited our friends and scurried throughout the house searching frantically for the fugitive turtle. I remember climbing to the top of the shelves in my closet and inspecting the highest corners. Never mind that they were six feet from the floor. Passion overcomes logic during an intense search. You never know where the lost may be so you search everywhere. Yet, even with our persistent efforts which surely lasted a solid seven minutes, we discovered no turtle.

My mom was not pleased with that. Perhaps she was already imagining the putrid smell of rotting turtle wafting from a hard-to-reach place. In time, however, even she conceded defeat. That turtle was lost.

Days became a week. One week became two. Then one night, our family was watching the old black and white box-television that fit into a built-in slot in the wall. Suddenly, someone spotted him. Moving slowly but deliberately from the tiny crack at the side of the T.V., like an escaped convict conceding defeat, our turtle returned to his cell. Apparently, he had vacationed among the dust-balls and dead bugs behind the T.V. for two weeks. Not a great time for him, yet what were his alternatives? Life as our pet was not enviable, even for a turtle.

His return was a time of rejoicing for us. Our wayward turtle had been found. With celebration, we put him back in his kidney-shaped bowl where he lived about as well as a turtle could expect to live . . . at least at our house.

A Sudden Shift in Priorities

If a prodigal turtle can shift our priorities, a lost person can prompt even more change. Lostologists have observed that when someone is lost, new priorities emerge instantly for those who must mount the search. Lostology Law #16 states this truth: a search becomes your consuming priority. In reality, it can be no other way.

If you received a call saying someone you love was missing, your priorities would change in a flash:

- An important meeting? It would have to wait.

- A presentation prepared for months? Sorry, new priorities.

- A vacation to Hawaii? No way. Out of the question.

In such a crisis, everything in our priority system resets to zero. One priority demands total attention: find the one who is lost.

Model Priorities

Jesus' lifestyle communicated the priority He gave to searching for the lost. On the morning after an exhausting day of ministry, Jesus got up early to spend time alone in prayer. When the crowd began to clamor for Jesus to meet their needs, the disciples went looking for Him. They knew what Jesus should do, and they were prepared to tell Him. "Everyone is looking for you!" they said. Their implication? Forget this prayer business and get back into action with people. The crowd must be top priority.

As usual, Jesus was unimpressed with their plans for His life. His response was classic: "Let us go somewhere else—to the nearby villages—so I can preach there also. That is why I have come" (Mark 1:38).

The disciples did not know Jesus very well at this point. In time, they learned that searching for the lost or training others to share in the search was Jesus' top priority. He refused to let anything or anyone distract Him.

Jesus' stories about the lost sheep and the lost coin in Luke 15 illustrate a shift in priorities:

- Undoubtedly, the shepherd was looking forward to other tasks or to an evening of rest as he counted his flock. But as his tally entered the nineties, he sensed something was wrong. One sheep was missing. Instantly, his plans changed. Securing the ninety-nine, he headed out to search for the prodigal sheep. One missing sheep changed his plans and shifted his priorities.

- The woman with the lost coin would have had many other things to do. But when she noticed that one of her prized coins was missing, she placed everything else on hold. She focused on a new objective: finding the lost coin. She meticulously swept her house, looking in hidden nooks and obscure crannies. The plans she had set previously were forgotten. A lost valuable changed her focus and altered the way she spent her day.

When a search is necessary, that search becomes the consuming priority. Everything in Jesus' life and teaching affirms this foundational truth of lostology.

DETERMINING CHURCH PRIORITIES

All of us struggle with competing priorities. Multiple demands clamor for top spot on our To-Do lists. It happens when Christians work together to set the priorities for their churches.

Our church in Oregon was established as a "search and rescue" church. From the beginning, we understood that we existed to reach lost people for Christ. We communicated this priority to all who became members of the church. To be with us was to join the search team. Over time, however, some in our church began to question that focus.

One day, a key leader said to me in frustration, "Sometimes, I feel like we're a church for people who aren't here." As soon as she said it, I thought, "She's right. We started this church for people without Christ and without a church. Nothing has changed that mission." Her statement stimulated my thinking over the next months. That year, on our church's anniversary, I entitled my state-of-the-church sermon "The Church for People Who Aren't Here." That sermon became a defining moment for many in our ministry—especially for me.

As a church, we did not exist for ourselves. We came together as Christians to search for those who were not there yet. That was our mission, our reason for existence. Perhaps not all Christians are called to be part of a church focused on reaching the lost. Perhaps evangelism is not the driving priority in every church. For us, it was.

That priority was costly for us. Some christians felt they could not get their spiritual needs met if we continued to focus on the lost. So they left. We did not blame them for leaving but we hated to see them go because they were vital to our team. Still, we were unwilling to shift the priorities to which God had called us. The search was top of the list. For us, that was non-negotiable.

Living with the Struggle

Essential elements for spiritual growth like personal time with God, Bible study, prayer, worship, ministry, and fellowship with believers all lay claim to our time. Since evangelism, by definition, focuses on people who are not in our midst, they cannot plead for the search to remain central. As a result, most churches move evangelism down the list. Most do so unintentionally. Yet the net result is the same: we do other things rather than searching for the lost.

The same thing happens in our personal lives. We never say, "Evangelism is unimportant." We simply raise the priority of other things, secular and spiritual, until there is no time left to share our faith.

Staying in Focus

Keeping an appropriate focus on reaching the lost is a constant challenge. Here are some practical steps that can help:

- Keep a prayer list of lost people you know and pray for them. Ask God to give you an opportunity to do something that helps those people move a step closer to Jesus.

- Carry a gospel tract with you. Simple booklets like "The Bridge to Life,"[6] "How to Have a Full and Meaningful Life,"[7] and "The Four Spiritual Laws"[8] are excellent tools you can use when talking to others about Christ. Carrying a tract helps you be ready to share your faith when the opportunity arises. The tract itself will serve as a tangible reminder that you are actively seeking opportunities to talk with others about Christ.

- Memorize a presentation of the gospel and review it regularly. The presentations in Continuing Witness Training and Evangelism Explosion are excellent.

- Participate in the outreach program of your church. If your church does not have an ongoing outreach program, volunteer to contact people who visit your church so you can talk to them about their relationship with Christ. Committing yourself to participate in outreach on a regular basis ensures you will keep evangelism as a priority in your schedule.

Evangelism is so challenging and the need so compelling, we must intentionally rank it high on our list of spiritual priorities. Without a top priority, we will find ourselves passing through years of our lives without ever talking with anyone about Christ. As lostologists, we must commit ourselves to keeping evangelism a focus in our lives. The "people who aren't there" desperately need us.

THE LOSTOLOGY LAB

- Recall a time when you lost something that caused you to change your plans so you could look for the item. Why did that lost item become top priority on your To-Do list?

- How do you determine how you will spend your time each day? If you keep a To-Do list, what criteria do you use to place items as top priorities?

- How do you adjust your To-Do list as you go through the day? What has to happen for you to alter your schedule based on new priorities?

- Imagine one of your loved ones was missing. How would the disappearance change the way you spent your time? How long would the change in your schedule continue?

- How do you deal with the pressure of competing priorities? When your choice is between two things that are both good and important, how do you decide what to do?

- Read Mark 1 and focus especially on verse 38. What impact do you think Jesus' time alone in prayer had on His schedule decisions?

- Have you found that spending time in Bible study and prayer helps you keep your priorities in order and enables you to make better decisions about how you spend your time? If so, name specific ways your personal devotional time with God helps you set priorities and live by them?

- If someone analyzed your calendar and To-Do lists for the last four weeks, what would they say your priorities have been?

- Do your priorities match the priorities you feel God wants you to have? If not, what changes will you need to make? Are you willing to make these changes?

COMING NEXT: TURNED AROUND BACKWARDS

Why is it so many Christians experience such poor results as they try to talk with others about Christ? The answer may be in how they approach the search. It is easy to start backwards and end up tied in a knot. We will untie this knot in our next chapter.

The Lost-Centered Search

As surely as I live, declares the Sovereign LORD . . .
my shepherds did not search for my flock
but cared for themselves rather than for my flock . . .
Ezekiel 34:8

Lostology Law #17
A search is always lost-centered, not searcher-centered.

See if you can place yourself in the following scene:

Hearing that a little girl named Amanda has been lost in the woods outside of town, you respond to the call for volunteer searchers. When you arrive at the base camp for the search, you're shocked by what you see.

Along the edge of the woods people have parked motor homes and travel trailers. Clusters of volunteers sit in lawn chairs around roaring fires in the common areas between the campsites. On the grills, steaks are cooking. Music plays. Laughter fills the air.

Those sitting around the fires occasionally look at maps. A few of the men tell stories of searches they have been part of in the past. Occasionally, the search coordinator walks to the edge of the woods and calls out, "Amanda. Amanda. Come here if you can hear me." Then he walks back to the group by the fire.

Outraged, you walk up to him and say, "What are you doing? You can't just sit here. That little girl is lost out there. Why aren't you looking for her?"

similar to football team from Maxwell

The head searcher seems confused. "Hold it, now," he says. "We've all made quite a sacrifice to be here already. We had to drive our rigs out here and set up camp. Some folks drove three hours. Now's the time to eat and relax. Don't worry. We'll keep our eyes open. Who knows? We may just see that little girl."

What is wrong with this scene? It is searcher-centered. The focus is on the searchers, their comfort and their convenience. In contrast, a true search is always lost-centered.

As with most of the laws of lostology, Law #17 is self-evident: a search is always lost-centered . . . not searcher-centered. Unfortunately, the truth we see so clearly in the story of Amanda is not applied to evangelism by many Christians and churches.

TRUTH YOU ALREADY KNOW

If that little girl, Amanda, were missing, you would know what to do even if you had never helped with a search before. You would find out all you could about her:

- What does she look like?

- What was she wearing?

- When did someone last see her?

- How much does she weigh?

- How tall is she?

- What does she like to do?

- What kinds of games does she like to play?

With every question, you would shift your perspective until you could think the little girl's thoughts. "Where would she go?" you would ask yourself. You would move out into the woods, calling her name, looking for any signs that she had been in the area. Noticing every trail and ledge, you would evaluate the chances of her going that way? Your attention would be fixed on one thing—that little girl. You would be Amanda-centered. Lost-centered.

CENTERED ON THE LOST

Jesus ordered His life around lost people. Rather than sit in a Lay-Z-Boy with the religious types, He left the comfort zone. Jesus went to the people. When they saw He was approachable, the people came to him:

- Prostitutes sought Jesus when they needed help, sensing that He was a man who would help, not hurt them.

- Tax collectors, the group most hated by the Jews, felt so comfortable with Jesus that they invited Him to parties as an honored guest.

- Those suffering from leprosy—the social scourge of that day—made their way to Jesus after hearing that He loved rather than rejected people with their disfiguring disease.

- Crowds of common people followed Jesus wherever He went. Lugging their needs with them, they dogged Jesus' path in hope that He would touch their lives with the miraculous.

Jesus' lost-centered life angered His critics. With indignation, they climbed onto their silly soapboxes and leveled a charge at Him, a charge He wore as a badge of honor. "That's Jesus," they scoffed, "the friend of tax collectors and sinners." He was. The critics spoke the truth.

Describing His work to these critics, Jesus said, "I'm a spiritual physician. Does it not make sense that I go to the sick rather than stay with the well?" The compelling logic of that argument only confused the spiritual elite. So Jesus continued to live with the people. Rather than wait for them to come to Him, He moved in their circles. Jesus lived a lost-centered life.

A NEW CENTER FOR LIFE

As I intensified my friendships with lost people, I made some major adjustments in my life. For the first time, I decided to join secular people on their social turf.

When they invited me to parties, I went. Honestly, much about those settings made me uncomfortable. The refreshments, the conversation, everything was very different from life in the church Fellowship Hall. In those social settings, I met and talked with more lost people than I had encountered in all my previous years of church visitation.

Besides going to parties, I joined civic clubs and business organizations. I enrolled in community training events and participated in service projects.

My life shifted dramatically. Gone were the days of a comfortable searcher-centered lifestyle. All along the way, I met and talked with lost people. I am not sure how well I did, but I knew I was doing the right things because I was uncomfortable . . . they weren't. It was the opposite of the normal church setting in which I felt comfortable while my secular friends had to adjust.

At parties, civic clubs, and community meetings, I had to change and adapt. How awkward I felt. Was this how these non-Christians felt when they came to church for the first time? I began to suspect it was.

MAKING THE CHANGE

In the past, most of us in the church assumed that lost people in attendance should adapt to our ways. We gave little thought to how they felt or how our actions impacted them. Today, many churches are taking a hard look at the way they "do church." Rather than settling for a searcher-centered existence, these churches are becoming lost-centered. As they make this shift, they refuse to compromise the message of the gospel. They do strive, however, to set aside unnecessary barriers that hinder the lost from hearing the gospel.

The changes that need to be made will vary from church to church. The key is not methods. The most significant shift is a changed attitude. Churches that become sensitive to the seekers in their midst will find, in time, that there are more seekers in their midst. When you're lost-centered, you find more lost people.

A SEARCHER-FOCUSED PARABLE

Frank Voight wrote a classic story called "The Lifesaving Station."[9] This simple parable illustrates how easily we can shift from being lost-centered to searcher-centered:

> On a dangerous seacoast where shipwrecks often occur was a crude, little lifesaving station. The building was just a hut, and there was only one boat. The few devoted members kept a constant watch over the sea. With no thought for themselves, they went out, day or night, searching tirelessly for the lost. So many lives were saved by the wonderful little station that it became famous.

Some of those who were saved, and various others in the surrounding area, wanted to become associated with the station and gave of their time, money, and effort for the support of its work. New boats were bought, and new crews were trained. The little lifesaving station grew.

Some of the new members of the lifesaving station were unhappy because the building was crude and poorly equipped. They felt that a more comfortable place should be provided as the first refuge of those saved from the sea. So they replaced the emergency cots with beds and put better furniture in an enlarged building.

Now the lifesaving station became a popular gathering place for its members, and they redecorated it beautifully and furnished it exquisitely because they used it as a club.

Fewer members were now interested in going to sea on lifesaving missions so they hired crews to do this work. The lifesaving motif still prevailed in the club decoration, however, and a symbolic lifesaving boat dominated the room where initiation took place.

About this time, a large ship was wrecked off the coast, and the hired crew brought in boat loads of cold, wet, and half-drowned people. They were dirty and sick; some had black skin, and some had yellow skin. The beautiful club was considerably messed up. So the property committee immediately had a shower house built outside the club where victims of shipwrecks could be cleaned up before coming inside.

At the next meeting, a split took place in the club membership. Most of the members wanted to stop the lifesaving activities as being unpleasant and a hindrance to the normal life of the club. Some members insisted on lifesaving as their primary purpose and pointed out that they still were called a lifesaving station. They finally were voted down, however, and told that if they wanted to save the lives of various kinds of people who were shipwrecked in those waters, they could begin their own lifesaving station down the coast. They did.

As the years went by, the new station experienced the same changes that had occurred in the old. It evolved into a club, and yet another lifesaving station was founded. History continued to repeat itself; and if you visit that coast today, you will find a number of exclusive clubs along that shore. Shipwrecks are still frequent in those waters. But most people drown.

STAYING LOST-CENTERED

A search is always lost-centered, not searcher-centered. How easily that focus can shift. As lostologists, we must guard against this insidious shift in our lives and in our churches. Here are some ways you can be lost-centered. Perhaps you can use this list to evaluate your life, your church, your Sunday School class or small group to determine if you need to take any corrective action:

- Go to the lost rather than expecting the lost to come to you. Christians should take the initiative rather than waiting for the non-Christians to take the first step.

- Meet the physical and emotional needs of the lost as well as their spiritual needs. Non-Christians will respond more readily to the words of the gospel after they have seen it lived out in ministry.

- Value non-Christians as people and seek to develop relationships with them. Never view them as your "evangelism project." No one wants to be your project.

- Lead your church or small group to devote time and resources to reaching the lost. Guard against the insidious tendency to spend all your time and resources on the Christians who are already part of the church.

- Join with other Christians in learning about lost people. Develop your skills as a lostologist so you can understand more about how non-Christians think and feel. Communicate what you learn to other Christians so they can be more effective as they share their faith.

- Work with your church and small group leaders to make it easy for non-christians to explore their beliefs in your church. Make sure new people feel welcome. Include them in the fellowship activities. Help them participate in Bible studies and discussions. Guard against confusing Christian jargon or referring to theological concepts without explanation.

- Lovingly challenge your non-Christian friends to commit their lives to Christ. Give them time, but do not allow them to become comfortable and stop making progress in their spiritual quests. In love, urge them to become Christians.

Unless we take specific steps to remain lost-centered, we will begin the subtle shift illustrated in the story, "The Lifesaving Station." We must not allow this story to remain a modern day parable of our searcher-centered lives and searcher-centered churches.

THE LOSTOLOGY LAB

- Review the story of Amanda in the beginning of this chapter. How would you respond if you had been in that situation? What would you have said to the people coordinating the search? What would you have done?

- How would you describe the difference between being lost-centered and being searcher-centered?

- Jesus lived a lost-centered life. From what you know about His life, what specific things did Jesus do because He was lost-centered?

- Do you think most Christians or churches are lost-centered or searcher-centered in the way they approach evangelism? Why?

- Up until now, have you been lost-centered or searcher-centered? What have you done or failed to do which causes you to place yourself in that category?

- If you wanted to become lost-centered, what specific changes would you need to make in your life? Do you want to make those changes? Are you going to make those changes?

- What does the story, "The Lifesaving Station," suggest to you about the forces that cause Christians to become searcher-centered rather than lost-centered? What subtle forces did you see at work in the people in the story? In what ways do you see these same forces at work in your life and in your church?

COMING NEXT: URGENCY REQUIRED

A sense of urgency always accompanies a search. However, what if people search without urgency? What does that tell us? We will explore this question next.

Race Against Time

Just as man is destined to die once,
and after that to face judgment . . .
Hebrews 9:27

Lostology Law #18
A search is urgent because the lost are in danger.

The Timberline Lodge straddles a line between trees and bare rock near the summit of Mt. Hood. Below it, forests of Douglas Firs lock limbs to form an evergreen wall all the way to Portland. Above the lodge, an ancient glacier sculpts the rock that forms the grand mount's peak. Climbers challenge the mountain regularly, trekking to the summit ridge then back to Timberline Lodge to tell conqueror's tales around crackling fires.

Twelve additional climbers planned to conquer Mt. Hood in May of 1986. Three adults and nine high school students left Timberline Lodge for an ascent to the peak. The weather had been questionable, but a break in storm fronts suggested they could complete their climb as planned.

Several hours into their arduous adventure, the weather changed. The storm systems regrouped and attacked with vengeance. Strong winds whipped, and blowing snow disoriented the climbers. The tiny band struggled to regain their bearings so they could retreat to Timberline.

Some of the students began to suffer from hypothermia. In desperation, their leader made the decision to build a snow cave for those who couldn't continue the descent. Three members went for help. Nine stayed behind.

Eventually, the three climbers reached the lodge. Search and rescue operations began immediately. But by that time, the storm's fury hindered the search efforts. Knowing what was at stake, emergency crews endured extreme conditions to continue their search. In spite of their efforts, it was three days before they found the tiny snow cave.

By the time the searchers arrived, it was too late. Only one of the climbers inside the cave was alive.

A FIELD OF EXTREMES

Lostology is a peculiar discipline. The field ranges from the humorous to the heartbreaking. It is fun to think about times we have been lost and reflect on the lessons learned in those embarrassing situations. We chuckle as we recall lost rings and fugitive turtles. Memories of the searches bring a smile years later. Lostology does have a light side.

There is, of course, another side . . . an intense and painful side. Here, lostology confronts truths learned in some of life's hardest moments: the search for lost people.

As lostologists, we face these truths, reflect on them, and use them to challenge our understanding of evangelism. Lostology Law #18 affirms one of these painful truths: A search is urgent because the lost are in danger.

No one had to tell the search team on Mt. Hood that their work was urgent. They knew it. The lost climbers were in grave danger. For that reason, the rescue team braved the storm and risked their lives to look for the climbers. Time was precious. The lost must be found. Fear of what would happen if their efforts were unsuccessful drove the searchers on. Others' lives depended on the success of their search so they risked their lives attempting to save others.

Lostology raises tough questions. Here is one: Do we believe searching for those who are lost spiritually is as urgent as searching for lost climbers? Most of us don't—at least we don't live as if we do. Jesus did.

JESUS' URGENT AGENDA

Urgency marked Jesus' life. Every action moved Him closer to His goals. Every decision reflected His ultimate priorities. Jesus lived life on a search and rescue mission. Jesus, more than we ever can, understood the spiritual stakes.

HEAVEN AND HELL

Jesus knew the reality of eternity. As a result, He taught about heaven and hell and the way our lives now impact our future in eternity.

In the parable of the rich man and Lazarus (Luke 16:19-31), Jesus communicated the torment of hell and the reward of heaven. Two characters marked the alternatives. In life, the rich man had all. Lazarus, the beggar, had nothing. In eternity, the roles reversed.

From hell, the rich man called out to Father Abraham to have pity on him. The once wealthy man begged for Lazarus to dip the tip of his finger in water and cool his, the rich man's, tongue. The man who had enjoyed so much in life was now in agony from the fire. What a vivid picture of the torment of hell.

Later in the story, Father Abraham explained to the rich man that Lazarus could not come to him. "Between us and you a great chasm has been fixed, so that those who want to go from here to you cannot, nor can anyone come over from there to us." What a vivid picture of the finality of eternal punishment.

THE CROSS

Jesus also understood the reality of the cross. Throughout His earthly ministry, the cross loomed in His thinking—a piercing reminder of the seriousness of sin. In the later half of His ministry, He spoke about the cross to His disciples, preparing them for what would occur:

> Again He took the Twelve aside and told them what was going to happen to Him. "We are going up to Jerusalem," he said, "and the Son of Man will be betrayed to the chief priests and teachers of the law. They will condemn Him to death and will hand Him over to the Gentiles who will mock Him and spit on Him, flog Him and kill Him. Three days later He will rise." (Mark 10:33-34)

URGENT BUSINESS

The cross, heaven, and hell—these spiritual realities enabled Jesus to live life with eternity in mind. This eternal mindset allowed Him to leave crowds who needed Him and move on to new areas where the gospel must be preached. Eternal truths kept Him constantly in search mode. Nothing distracted Him. No one sidetracked Him. Jesus focused on the search and the ultimate rescue.

A DISTURBING LACK OF URGENCY

Why do many Christians lack urgency in their search for lost people? Here are three possible reasons:

- Some question whether non-Christians are really lost. The world's cafeteria line of religions offers some appealing and plausible entrees. Some Christians begin to question secretly if Jesus is the *only* way to God. "Even if people travel different paths, don't all roads lead to God in the end?" they ask. That idea impacts their attitudes toward evangelism. If people are not really lost, the need to get involved in an intense spiritual search dissolves.

- Others wonder if the lost are in ultimate danger. Some Christians lull themselves out of urgency with the thought that somehow, after people die, God will make it possible for them to go to heaven. They reason that even if God punishes people for a season, surely He will not punish them for eternity. If you don't think people are in everlasting danger, it is easy to throttle back on any search efforts.

- Some Christians toy with the idea that those who die without Christ will simply die without any future life whatsoever. In this view, missing out on eternity is the punishment for rejecting Christ. Of course, the lost don't know they are missing out because they are dead. This idea helps Christians say, "Well, they got what they deserved. They miss eternity, but at least they won't have to endure hell's torment." Once again, this perspective neutralizes urgency and fuels complacency. The need for a search dims.

No matter how plausible or appealing these views may be, they deny biblical reality. These views offer false hope. That is why few evangelical Christians admit they hold these beliefs. Put on the spot, they affirm that Jesus is the only way to God and that those without Christ will spend eternity in hell. Still the undercurrent of doubt remains.

Christians sing the words—we affirm the biblical truths about evangelism. But our lives do not play the music—we do not share our faith with lost people. Somewhere, somehow, something has dulled our sense of urgency. So we search infrequently and without urgency. We must ask why.

An Urgency Transfusion

A friend of mine has an intriguing habit. On a regular basis he takes a sheet of paper and writes affirmations he holds central in His life. For example, one day he wrote, "I believe Jesus really is the Christ." Then throughout that day, he thought about that affirmation and drew it into focus in His life.

Another day he wrote, "I believe the Bible is God's word." That day he centered His thinking on the Bible and made that affirmation burn bright in His life once again.

Most Christians don't intentionally deny the fundamentals of our faith or embrace an errant doctrine. We simply lose spiritual focus. Spiritual Alzheimer's disease sets in and we forget things we have known for years.

A simple practice like my friend's affirmation sheet can help us discipline our thinking with central truths. As lostologists, we can use this practice to transfuse our spiritual system with urgency for evangelism. Why not start with these affirmations?

- Jesus is the only way to God.

- Every person deserves to hear about Jesus.

- I can tell others what Jesus has done for me.

- All who die without Christ will spend eternity in hell.

- I must tell others about God's gift of eternal life.

- Deep down, people long for a relationship with God.

- It is wrong to keep the good news about Jesus to myself.

Use one of these affirmations (or write one of your own) and focus on it for one full day. Pray about it. Think about it. Evaluate your life by it. The next day, move on to another affirmation and repeat the process. Continue this pattern for a full week. Ask God to rejuvenate your sense of urgency about sharing Christ with those around you. He will!

The Lostology Lab

- Review the story about the hikers lost on Mt. Hood in the beginning of this chapter. How would you have felt if you had been part of the search team that braved the storm to look for the hikers? What thoughts would have gone through your mind as you endured the bitter cold and risked your own life to search for the hikers? When you grew weary, cold, and discouraged, what would you have told yourself to keep going in your search effort?

- What impact did Jesus' awareness of the cross, heaven, and hell have on the urgency with which He lived His life and searched for the lost?

- Why do you think most Christians live without a sense of urgency about reaching the lost?

- What level of urgency do you feel personally about reaching the lost?

- What stops you from sharing your faith?

- If you were going to use the Affirmation Sheet exercise suggested in this chapter, with which affirmation on the list would you begin? Why? If you were going to add an affirmation of your own to the list, what would it be? Why would you add it?

COMING NEXT: SEARCH CONTROL

The urgency of a search should prompt us to action. But we must never confuse activity with accomplishment. How we begin the search effort and how we use the resources we have may ultimately determine our chances of success. Coordination becomes a key. We will tackle this topic as we begin Part Four of our study.

PART FOUR

Secrets of a Successful Search

Search Control Center

After this the Lord appointed seventy-two others
and sent them two by two ahead of Him to every town
and place where he was about to go. He told them,
"The harvest is plentiful, but the workers are few."
Luke 10:1-2

Lostology Law #19
Coordinate resources to maximize the search.

Our scoutmaster, Mr. Range, yelled for us to circle around him. Talk about a motley crew: twentysomething elementary-aged boys, grimy and stinky from the weekend campout, noisy and obnoxious. Bumping and pushing, poking and punching, we gathered around our leader.

"We have a missing scout," Mr. Range said solemnly. "We need to look for him."

Suddenly interested, we all asked, "Who's missing? Yeah, who's not here?"

Mr. Range said, "It's Squiffy."

Upon hearing of poor Squiffy's plight, all of us were touched by emotion. Sensitive as any group of little boys could be, we cut loose with a series of boisterous affirmations and assessments:

"Way to go, Squiffy. Yeah, way to go."

"Squiffy always gets lost."

"That Squiffy is so stupid."

"He probably got lost coming back from the latrine."

"No way. Squiffy probably fell in the latrine."

On and on we piped one wisecrack after another. Not your "dream team" for a search. But we were it—a bunch of knot-headed little boys and a few frustrated adult leaders.

Mr. Range had limited resources for his search effort. Strategy became supremely important. He could have said, "Boys, you all know what Squiffy looks like. Head out until you find him. Report back to me." We would have loved that. Of course, most of us would have gotten lost along with Squiffy.

No, Mr. Range was a wise leader of men . . . and goosey little boys. Immediately, he began to bark out instructions: "Men, let's stretch out in a line with about ten feet or so between each of us. Don't start until I tell you. Just stand there."

We began to position ourselves. Leaders interspersed themselves between every four to five boys. In the end, our search line stretched for several hundred feet through the forest.

From the center of the line, Mr. Range called out, "All right; let's go." On his order, we began to move forward, giggling, chucking rocks, messing around, occasionally calling out "Squiffy! Hey, Squiffy!"

Squiffy's dramatic rescue was anti-climactic. I didn't even see it. Someone else found Squiffy—not lost, but hiding in the woods because he was mad about something. The intense search and rescue mission only lasted a few minutes.

Before we knew it, we were back at camp loading up packs, muddy tents, and dirty dishes into the leaders' cars. Search completed, we headed home. Twentysome grungy little boys, a tired group of dedicated leaders, one wise scoutmaster . . . and Squiffy.

SPONTANEOUS COMBUSTION

The search for Squiffy that day was a coordinated effort. Many search efforts are more spontaneous and far less organized.

It happens when someone gets lost. The word spreads. Phones and doorbells ring as the news travels throughout the circle of concerned relatives and friends. People gather. A collective rush of adrenaline energizes the group. Action. Get with it. Do something . . . anything. Get moving. Find him. Look for her. Call back when you know something. Like a hornets' nest smacked with a rock, the searchers swarm helter-skelter in a frenzy of concern. The search begins, high on energy, low on coordination.

As students of lostology, we know that such spontaneous searches can be effective. Sometimes, such searchers find lost people. But not usually, and never if the search area is vast and the terrain rugged. Such high risk circumstances require more than activity. They demand coordination.

Lostology Law #19 encapsules the truth Mr. Range taught a group of men and little boys that day in the woods: coordinate your resources to maximize your search. Activity and good intentions are not enough. Effective coordination of resources and energy will determine the success or failure of the rescue effort.

In evangelism, we desperately need to coordinate our efforts so we can maximize our results. How easily we miss this basic law of lostology and rush out into the world with evangelistic activity that lacks collective impact. Fortunately, Jesus' life provides a model that helps us develop a coordinated approach to evangelism.

MODEL COORDINATION

As we have already observed, Jesus spent His years of earthy ministry in an intense spiritual search and rescue mission. He moved into a lost world to help lost people find God.

Jesus was an incredibly effective personal searcher. No one surpassed His search skills. But the key to Jesus' success was not His personal contact with the lost. Instead, Jesus invested the majority of His time gathering, training, and coordinating a long term search and rescue force.

JESUS' MASTER PLAN

Robert Coleman, in his classic book, *The Master Plan of Evangelism*, makes this insightful statement:

> Jesus was a realist. He fully realized the fickleness of depraved human nature as well as the Satanic forces of this world amassed against humanity, and in this knowledge He based His evangelism on a plan that would meet the need. The multitudes of discordant and bewildered crowds were potentially ready to follow Him, but Jesus individually could not possibly give them the personal care they needed. His only hope was to get men imbued with His life who would do it for Him. Hence, He concentrated Himself upon those who were to be the beginning of this leadership. Though He did what He could to help the multitudes, He had to devote Himself primarily to a

141

few men, rather than the masses, in order that the masses could at last be saved. This was the genius of his strategy.[10]

Jesus provided a model for us, a master strategy we can follow. In just over three years, He enlisted a group of unlikely leaders and spent time with them until their lives were marked by His values. Jesus broadened their base of experience and increased their skills. Through progressively challenging circumstances, He pushed His men to their limits and beyond, stretching their faith and building their confidence in God. Instruction was on-the-job, not in the classroom. One of their training assignments in spiritual search and rescue work included the following instructions:

> Calling the Twelve to Him, He sent them out two by two and gave them authority over evil spirits. These were His instructions: "Take nothing for the journey except a staff—no bread, no bag, no money in your belts. Wear sandals but not an extra tunic. Whenever you enter a house, stay there until you leave that town. And if any place will not welcome you or listen to you, shake the dust off your feet when you leave, as a testimony against them." They went out and preached that people should repent. (Mark 6:6-13)

The disciples embarked on their mission then reported back to Jesus. They told of the things they experienced and the supernatural work God did through them. Jesus affirmed them and continued to train and prepare them. Through crisis and pain, through joy and celebration, He molded them and equipped them for their mission—His Great Commission.

Multiplying the Search Force

Eventually, these men became the ultimate search and rescue force. After Jesus' death and resurrection, these evangelism veterans moved out and continued the search. More importantly, they enlisted and trained others until Jesus' search force extended to the ends of the earth.

What if Jesus had not taken time to enlist, train, and coordinate the search efforts of others? What if He had simply told His disciples: "There are lots of lost people out there. Go get them."

Activity? No doubt. Enthusiastic searching? Probably. But not success . . . at least not long term success. Jesus, the great Lostologist, knew that you coordinate a search to maximize your results. How we need to follow His model in the church today.

COLLECTIVE IMPACT

Our church in Portland centered around core organizational units called Community Groups. These small groups, drawn to each other through affinity and shared interests, joined together to grow in faith and reach others for Christ. At their best, these groups provided a wonderful means for people to work together in search and rescue activities which maximized their effectiveness.

Community Groups planned activities that were designed to create positive settings for new people to get acquainted and receive initial exposure to Christianity. New Christians knew other seekers, so they invited their friends. Seasoned spiritual veterans added their maturity and insights to help answer spiritual questions. The social types developed the activities. The organizers planned the events. Quiet people worked in the background. The extroverts worked the crowd. Everyone worked together.

Effective Community Groups accomplished more in their evangelistic searches through coordinating their efforts than any member could have done alone. Spiritual mathematics occurred: adding individual strengths together yielded multiplied influence.

A PART IN THE PLAN

Every Christian can and should be involved in reaching people for Christ. This does not mean, however, that we all work in the same way or bring the same gifts to the search effort. Yet when we all use the special gifts God has given us, and use them cooperatively, our collective impact increases the chance of successful search efforts.

Every Sunday School class, every small group, and every church can become a team that works together to seek and find the lost. When cooperation occurs, everyone benefits. The searchers receive the satisfaction of participating in an effective evangelistic activity. The lost receive the ultimate benefit: they get found!

Here are a few steps you can take to work together with others in evangelism:

- Build on the enthusiasm and contacts of new Christians in your group. Team the new Christians with longtime Christians. Working together, the new Christians can invite their lost friends to the group, and the longtime Christians can help supply answers to spiritual questions. If your group does not have any new Christians in it, pray and work and trust God to enable you to lead someone to Christ. Most groups experience greater opportunities for effective evangelism when they can build on the contacts of the new Christians among them. Plus, the changed lives and vibrant faith of new Christians encourage spiritual veterans like nothing else can.

- Identify and build on the collective strengths of the group. God has gifted everyone in your group with spiritual gifts and talents. Learn enough about each other to identify those gifts and talents and plan activities with these in mind.

- Remember that God wants to use you *because of* who you are, not *in spite of* who you are. As you plan your outreach activities, ask this question: What types of people can people like us reach for Christ? Usually, you are most effective reaching certain types of people—either people like you or members of a different race or nationality for whom you have special concern.

- Work together using your collective gifts in ministry. Evangelism often results from ministry. If you are not sure how to begin in evangelism, begin with ministry. Meet the needs of people in your community, and opportunities to share your faith will come. Working in ministry is a wonderful way to involve people in evangelism who are frightened by the idea of talking to others about their faith. These people can share their faith through acts of service in Jesus' name. Explain to those you serve that everything your group does springs from your commitment to Christ and your desire for others to know Him.

- Plan group fellowship activities and invite others to join you. Some non-Christians are surprised to discover that Christians are "normal" people who enjoy having fun. Celebrate the joy you have in Christ. Demonstrate distinctive Christian fellowship. Before long, your non-Christian friends will be curious about Jesus—the One who draws your lives together.

All of us are called to share our faith. Evangelism is not an add-on feature of the Christian life. Evangelism is a matter of obedience. For most of us, working as part of a search and rescue team provides the ideal way to reach others for Christ. As lostologists, we know the importance of coordinating our efforts to maximize our impact. Now We need to join with others and seek the lost together.

The Lostology Lab

- Recall a time when you lost an item and had to look for it alone. How did you feel while you were searching? How effective were you? Now recall a time when you lost something but others helped you search for it. How did you feel knowing that others were searching with you? How effective was your search?

- Why do you think a search activity that is high on energy but low on coordination tends to be ineffective? What does coordination add to the search effort that makes such a difference?

- What difference would it have made if Jesus had personally worked to reach the lost but had never trained His disciples to search?

- Have you ever been part of a small group of Christians who worked together to reach others for Christ? What made the group effective? What part did you play in the group's activities in evangelism?

- If you are in a Sunday School class or small group right now that is not involved in outreach, what needs to change for that group to be effective in reaching the lost? What can you do to help your group reach out to non-Christians?

- Have you ever been part of a group of longtime Christians that added a new Christian to its fellowship? What sort of impact did the new Christian have on the life of the group?

- In what ways can teams of Christians successfully involve people in evangelism who would have struggled on their own to tell lost people about Christ?

Coming Next: On Your Guard

Search and rescue is hard work. Rarely is success quick or easy. Often, the most important question searchers must ask themselves is "What will it take to stop us?" Many times, the force that stops the search effort takes the searchers by surprise.

TWENTY

The Discouragement Disease

Therefore we do not lose heart.
Though outwardly we are wasting away,
yet inwardly we are being renewed day by day.
2 Corinthians 4:16

Lostology Law #20
Discouragement threatens a successful search.

Discouragement is like the flu. It infects intensive search efforts from the beginning. Invisible emotional bacteria multiply and spread until searchers ache and burn and long for relief. This flu has diverse, sometimes subtle symptoms: loss of hope, fatigue and despair. Weakened by discouragement's relentless attack, searchers begin to say "There's no reason to continue; we won't find them." Discouragement nearly undermined the search for Patricia Lidrich and Katherine Spencer in April 1991.

The two set out on Saturday, April 6, for a hike in the Horsetail Falls area of the Columbia River Gorge—the dividing line between Oregon and Washington. No one knew they were missing until Monday when Lidrich did not report for work.

A search began Monday night and continued through the day Tuesday as rescue teams scoured the trails in the heavily wooded and hilly area. But Tuesday evening, officials called off the search, prepared to treat the case as a missing persons investigation. "We went over the high-probability areas over and over again and found nothing to lead us on," a spokesman said.

At that point, Spencer's son and other relatives began planning their own search. Officials warned them about the danger of such an effort but said they understood why the family wanted to keep searching. Relatives wiped tears from their eyes as they left the search area Tuesday night. The brother of Katherine Spencer said he was disappointed the official search ended so soon. "I think a person deserves more than one day's search," he said.

THE SECOND CHANCE SEARCH

It is a good thing some people refused to give up. The *Oregonian* newspaper carried the rest of the story on the front page on Friday, April 12, 1991. Here is what happened.

In spite of the official decision to end the ground search, volunteers and the 304th Aerospace Rescue and Recovery Squadron continued searching. On Thursday, while surveying an area searchers had investigated before, a helicopter pilot spotted the two women waving a blanket. The crew rescued them, ending a five day endurance drill that included freezing temperatures, isolation, and meager rations. The women said later that they were down to thirty raisins and some applesauce when the pilot rescued them. In spite of their ordeal, both women were in high spirits and good condition.

NEWS TRAVELS FAST

Back at the school where one of the women taught, a celebration erupted Thursday morning as news spread that their teacher was safe. At the gorge, the brother of one of the women had waited quietly in the trailhead parking lot all day Tuesday and Wednesday to hear word of his sister's fate. Waiting there again Thursday morning, he said he had little hope that the women would be found alive. But soon he was grinning and wiping away tears of joy, saying the good news made the wait worthwhile. He quickly credited the searchers who had helped hunt for the two women. "These people who came out and helped," he said, "they're incredible."

ENDING TOO SOON

We can understand why people end search efforts too soon. After working and sweating, and searching and trying with no apparent success, discouragement sets in. Discouragement whispers lethal lies:

- It's really no use.

- You'll never find them.

- You might as well quit.

Lies they are. But lies can persuade. Lies can make us quit. By quitting too soon, we may scuttle a search that could have been successful. What would have happened if the searchers in Oregon had stopped their search too soon? We know the answer. That is why lostology identifies a key law: discouragement threatens a successful search.

The discouragement disease lies dormant in every search effort. The disease flourishes in every search that extends over time. Understanding the pathology of this emotional infection allows us to immunize ourselves against it. Even with knowledge and prevention, discouragement persists. Those who search must learn to manage discouragement. There is no alternative.

LONG DISTANCE PACE

Jesus' interaction with his disciples provides an incredible model of discouragement management. How well Jesus understood the emotional toll their demanding work would have on his young leaders. Whipsawed emotions were an inherent part of their work with fickle crowds and persistent antagonists.

Through it all, Jesus monitored His disciples' emotional and physical health, intentionally pulling them away from the press of the crowd for time alone, time just with Him. Jesus knew He was training a group of long distance runners, not sprinters. He needed men with stamina, leaders who could go the distance.

The mission to which He called these men demanded emotional maturity and balance. He needed men who could resist the seductive acclaim of the crowd while rebounding from the debilitating accusations of opponents.

The disciples, Jesus' core search and rescue team, had to be a disciplined force who could sustain His mission for the long haul. So He trained them;

He paced them. He challenged; He corrected them. Under His watchful instruction and guiding love, these men built their emotional and spiritual reserves and prepared to move out in spiritual power to change the world.

THE ONE-WORD SUMMARY

If I had to sum up the years I worked with our church in Portland in one word, I could do so. One word captures the central emotion: discouragement. Not that our time in this ministry was negative. Those were positive, challenging days. Not that there were not times of joy—those were some of the best days of my life. But from the first Sunday, our days were peppered with discouragement.

Search efforts yielded fewer people than we had hoped. Strategies never worked as effectively as we had envisioned. Outside forces converged to make our task more difficult. Every week brought new obstacles. Disappointment stained every victory.

Discouragement took me by surprise. I was unprepared for the dulling impact discouragement could have. Looking back, I now understand why Dr. Howard Hendricks called discouragement "leukemia of the spirit." Discouragement saps energy, robs joy, and undermines confidence. All this and more we experienced in our battle with discouragement.

After a few years in the struggle, my wife and I discussed the powerful force discouragement had become in our lives. As we talked, we identified our key challenge: "The most important thing we will do is refuse to give up. We can succeed if we will not quit." That does not sound like a strong goal—to simply refuse to give up. But in the spiritual search and rescue trenches, refusing to quit is a daily battle requiring fresh commitment each morning.

In retrospect, I now know there were many ways I opened myself unnecessarily to discouragement. Unrealistic expectations, underestimating the challenge at hand, misunderstanding my personal gifts and the gifts of those who worked with me—these and other factors could have been adjusted with positive results. But a battle with discouragement was unavoidable.

COMMITMENT FOR THE LONG HAUL

When we challenge Christians to reach out to secular people and win them for Christ, we do well to talk to them about the exhilaration of the search and the joy of a successful rescue. But that is only part of the story. As they respond to the challenge and intentionally search on an ongoing basis, we must equip them to deal with discouragement.

Many Christians, gifted and potentially effective, have given up on evangelism. The inherent time required to reach secular people caused them to doubt their personal effectiveness in evangelism. They became discouraged. Discouragement bred doubt. They quit seeking the lost.

Many have given up on evangelism

We must decide from the beginning how we will manage discouragement because it is inevitable. Here are a few practical steps to help us get ready:

- Check your expectations. Recognize that it takes time to reach people for Christ. Secular adults have developed their values and ideas over many years. They will not change quickly, if at all. Take the long view. Be ready to sow seeds, cultivate, and wait for the harvest. Do not expect to harvest today what you plant today.

- Be yourself. Don't force yourself to share your faith according to a pattern prescribed by others. There are many effective methods of evangelism. Some will work for you; others will not. God made you and gifted you. He will use your unique personality, gifts, talents, and temperament to tell others about Jesus. Be available. Be prepared. God will use you.

- Gather together for encouragement and support. Do not try to do spiritual search and rescue work alone. Jesus gathered twelve people when He formed His team, and when He sent His disciples to the field, He sent them in pairs. As Christians, we need each other.

- Separate what you can do from what only God can do. You are called to search and to share. You cannot convict people of sin. You cannot cause people to seek God. Only God can draw people to Himself. Do not assume responsibility for God's part of the operation.

An airline pilot once described His job as hours of boredom punctuated by seconds of sheer terror. So it is with a search—hours of grueling, unproductive work punctuated by moments of pure joy when the lost are found. Often, they are not found. Basic training for the spiritual search must include discouragement management. It will come. We must not let it take us by surprise.

THE LOSTOLOGY LAB

Review the story about the two lost hikers at the beginning of this chapter. Answer these questions:

- What decision would you have made if you had been responsible for the search effort and the expense involved in continuing the search and rescue operation?

- How long do you think the volunteers would have continued to search if the women had not been found quickly? What lies would discouragement have begun to whisper to them?

- The brother of one of the women said, "I think a person deserves more than one day's search." What applications for evangelism can you draw from this statement?

- Jesus worked with His disciples to prepare them for discouragement. His primary strategy was to pull His men away from the crowds so they could spend personal time with Him. What role does your personal devotional time of prayer and Bible study have in discouragement management?

- When you become discouraged in your spiritual life, what helps you get going or keep going?

- Have you become discouraged and given up your attempts to share your faith? If so, with what you now know about lostology, what must you do to get involved in evangelism again?

- If God will help you, are you willing to persevere in spite of discouragement so you can share your faith with lost people? If so, tell God. Ask God to help you overcome discouragement and join His spiritual search and rescue team again.

COMING NEXT: SEARCHING WHILE STANDING STILL

We need to understand the many phases of a search. Once we do, we are better prepared to shift from an active to a less active phase. Sometimes, searching involves going. Other times, searching involves staying right where we are. In the next chapter, we will focus on the most misunderstood phase of the search.

Waiting While Searching

> But while he [the prodigal son] was still a long way off,
> his father saw him and was filled with compassion for him;
> he ran to his son, threw his arms around him and kissed him.
>
> Luke 15:20

Lostology Law #21
Waiting is part of searching.

My Grandmother Frachiseur ranked as a world class *wait-ERr*. Not the kind of waiter who brings you food in a restaurant. Grandmother *waited* for people to show up.

Having spent the majority of her life on a farm with a large family, much of my grandmother's life revolved around preparing meals and waiting for people to show up. Even after my grandfather died and Grandmother moved into town and lived alone, she often prepared big meals on Sunday "just in case" people dropped by. (They usually did!)

For Grandmother, waiting was an expression of love. What qualified her as one of the world's great wait-ers was that she extended her gift of waiting to unlikely people.

One weekend while I was in college, I returned to my parents' home and brought a friend with me, a fellow named Chris. Grandmother was also visiting that weekend. Chris and I enjoyed a wonderful time with her, stuffing ourselves on down-home, country cooking as only she could prepare.

That evening, Chris had plans that took him one place and I ended up going somewhere else. We told my parents and Grandmother we would be out late and not to worry.

Some time after midnight I returned home. Entering through the back door, I prepared to go upstairs to my bedroom. As I did, I noticed a light in the den. Curious, I walked in and noticed Grandmother sitting in the rocking chair, her head leaning forward, sound asleep.

As I came in, she woke up. "Grandmother," I said, "what are you doing out here?" She smiled and said, "Oh, I was just waiting up until you got home." We talked for a few minutes. I told her about my evening and then said I was going to bed.

She looked at me and said, "Is Chris home yet?" Puzzled, I replied, "No, he said he'd be home real late." She nodded as I moved toward the door, but she did not get up. "Aren't you going to bed, Grandmother?" I asked. "No," she replied, "I'd better wait up for Chris."

Over the years, I learned many things from my grandmother. None surpassed the lesson she taught me that night as she "waited up" for someone she had met that day for the first time. For her, waiting was not passive or inactive. Waiting was something that told other people "You are important; I love you." My grandmother believed everyone needed someone to keep the light on and wait up.

LIFE AS A *Wait-er*

Think of a time you waited for someone because of your concern:

- someone running late on a stormy night

- a teenager out on a date

- someone lost for whom you had exhausted your capacity to search

What does it mean to wait? By waiting, we communicate much about our attitudes and emotions. Waiting shows we are preoccupied with one who is not there. Waiting can be a subtle but powerful expression of love. When we no longer wait, we may show that hope or even love has dimmed.

Lostology focuses on the act of waiting. When we wait, we not only communicate love; we engage in an essential part of searching for the lost.

WAITING MISUNDERSTOOD

Jesus' story of the prodigal son tells us more about the father than it does about the son who left home. What did the prodigal's father do while his son was missing? Did he go and search for him? Did he try to persuade him to come home? We don't know. Jesus did not tell us.

We do know what the father was doing when his son appeared on the road heading home: the father was waiting. Coincidental timing? Did the father just happen to be there at the precise moment his son arrived? No way. What is more likely is that the father was there because that is where he spent much of his time while his son was gone.

So why did the father wait rather than search? That is the troubling question.

For the father, waiting was not passive. Waiting did not indicate a lack of concern. On the contrary, waiting simply showed that the father had accepted reality: there was nothing more he could do. He had to trust forces he could not control to carry his son home. If or until that happened, he did the one thing he could do. He expressed his love for his son by waiting. As long as he waited and watched, he nurtured the hope that one day his lost son would come home.

The father embodied Lostology Law #21: waiting is part of searching.

ACTIVELY WAITING

I will never forget Saturday night, March 12, 1988. As my former pastor used to say: "It hangs like a fishhook in the gray matter of my mind." (A gruesome analogy, but it describes the degree to which this memory lingers.) That was the night before the first service of our new church in Portland.

Almost a year of work had been completed. Thousands of people had been invited to attend. Volunteers from Texas and other churches in the northwest were prepared to help us conduct our first worship service for all who came the next morning.

My best friend, David Francis, was there leading the volunteer team from Texas and providing emotional support as only a best friend could. Together we debated how many chairs to set up in the auditorium, probing the theological implications if we set up too few chairs. (Would that be viewed as a lack of faith?) And as ardent pragmatists, we pondered the psychological impact of having several hundred chairs set up if only a handful of people showed up. (Would that be viewed as a sign of stupidity?) Profound questions. . . with elusive answers. We took our best shot with 250 chairs as the optimum balance of faith and pragmatism.

I did not sleep well that night. It didn't really matter, because it was a short night. We got up at 4:30 A.M. to begin preparing the facility for our first service at 9:00. For three hours we moved Sunday School equipment, silk plants, and chairs. We set up sound system equipment, tuned instruments, and completed all the other tasks necessary to prepare for the morning. A little past 8:00, we were ready. Everything looked great. There was nothing more we could do but wait.

I stared at the empty chairs lining the auditorium until my fears began to overcome me. *"What if no one shows up?"* I thought. Finally, I told David that I was going back to one of the classrooms. I felt helpless. All that could be done was done. It was now beyond my control.

About a quarter until 9:00, David stepped through the door. Tears filled his eyes as he smiled at me. "People are coming," he said. "They're really coming." And they did; 209 that first day.

The work and the wait was over. We were ready to begin a church. We had worked, and we had waited. Waiting was part of the work.

PART OF THE PLAN

As we seek to reach secular people for Christ, there are many steps we can take. We can work and build relationships. We can pray and probe and seek to meet needs. But with some people, we come to the point where we have done all that can be done. At that point, the waiting phase begins.

A VERY LONG WALK

On one occasion, a Christian leader went to visit a tribe of people in Africa. The people had anticipated the visit and were prepared to welcome their honored guest. While the leader was there, one of the children, a young boy, came up to her and handed her a beautiful shell. The woman looked at it and admired it. She smiled at the boy and said, "Thank you."

The interpreter looked at the shell, then explained that the shell was extremely rare and could only be found in an area several days walk from the village. The leader was stunned by the sacrifice the boy had made for her. She turned to the boy, and through the interpreter said, "You shouldn't have walked so far just to get me a gift."

The boy smiled, then responded in broken English, "Long walk part of gift."

EMBRACING WAITING

When we embrace waiting as part of evangelism, we make several positive affirmations about the waiting phase of a spiritual search:

- Coming to Christ will be a long process for some people, especially adults. Their journey to faith will take time, so we must be prepared to wait.

- Actively talking with lost friends about their commitment to Christ can become counterproductive after repeated discussions and rejections. Further discussion can create resentment and even damage relationships. In these cases, waiting may be the only productive action Christians can take.

- When we are willing to wait, we affirm that God is ultimately in control of everything. He can use a variety of people and means to reach our lost friends. We may be in a waiting phase while God moves someone else into their lives in a more active role.

- Waiting gives us time to pray. Prayer reminds us that evangelism is ultimately God's work. Only He can convict our lost friends of sin. Only God can draw lost people to Himself. Waiting reminds us that the process does not hinge on our activity. Reaching the lost is God's work from first to last. He simply gives us the privilege and responsibility of joining Him in the process.

- Waiting allows our faith to grow through testing. While waiting, we stretch our ability to expect what we cannot see and hope for what appears to be impossible. While waiting, we can affirm our confidence in God's power to do his work. Waiting give us the opportunity to get up every day—armed only with God's promises—and look down the road, expecting to see the prodigal come home.

PART OF THE GIFT

Searching is part of love's gift. When we search, we communicate to others that we love and value them. But waiting is also part of the gift. When the lost are found, we can say, "We searched for you." Then we can add, "We also waited for you."

When we searched, we revealed our love. When we waited, we revealed our expectations and the focus of our hearts. As lostologists, we know that waiting is part of searching. Often, the long wait is part of the gift.

THE LOSTOLOGY LAB

- Has there been a time when someone waited up for you as an expression of love and concern. How did you feel?

- Was there ever a time when you waited up for someone because you were concerned about their safety, but were powerless to do anything? How did you feel? What did you do? Would you classify your activity as passive or active? Why?

- When you read the story of the prodigal son prior to your study of lostology, how did you feel about the father's decision to stay at home rather than search for his son? Why did you believe he stayed home? What did you believe his actions communicated? Have you changed your views as a result of this study? If so, how?

- If waiting is part of the process of evangelism, how does this truth change the way you attempt to share your faith with lost friends and loved ones?

- How would you determine when it is appropriate to move into a waiting phase with a lost friend, rather than continuing to actively talk about Christ?

- Based on what you have learned about the waiting phase of evangelism, how will you make your waiting active rather than passive? How will you approach prayer? How will you use the waiting phase as an opportunity to develop your faith? How will you use waiting as a time to focus on God's work in reaching your lost friends and loved ones?

COMING NEXT: THE QUESTION OF SUCCESS

Is a search only successful when the lost are found? Or is there something intrinsically significant about the fact that people search for the lost? We will explore this question as we study the next law of lostology.

A Tragic End to a Successful Search

For God was pleased to have all his fullness dwell in him,
and through him to reconcile to himself all things . . .
by making peace through his blood, shed on the cross.
Colossians 1:19-20

Lostology Law #22
Successful searches do not always have happy endings.

It was a sad story in slow motion. A ranching family in a small community
was moving their herd of cattle to the winter grazing area. Working with
his father and other cowboys was a teenage boy—we'll call him Joe. One
afternoon, Joe headed back to camp alone on his horse. It was the last time
anyone saw him.

After initial efforts to find Joe were unsuccessful, the family, through
the local media, appealed for volunteers to help them search the wooded
hills and canyons of the area. Many did. For days the evening news
reported on their search effort. But Joe remained lost without a trace.

As days slipped into a week, the family's sense of urgency rose. Winter
was coming. If Joe was alive, he must be found soon or he would not be
found at all. The search continued. One week became two. No Joe. The
weather worsened. Volunteers slipped away, sensing they were no longer
looking for a boy; they were looking for a body.

Winter came. The snows fell. Still the family searched. The media carried their story a while longer. The father said they could not stop until they knew what had happened to their son. Their lonely search continued.

When the snows made additional searching impossible, the family gave up, but said they would begin again in the spring. They did. Months later a report filtered out to all who remembered the original story that a body had been found. It was Joe.

EVALUATING A SEARCH EFFORT

How would you evaluate the search for Joe? A success? Hardly. A family lost a son. Nothing could erase their pain nor change their sense of loss. They had searched, but they did not find their son alive. They failed. The search was unsuccessful. Or was it? Some facts challenge a simplistic assessment:

- A family's love for a lost son launched a massive search.

- Friends and volunteers joined the extensive search effort.

- Through the media, thousands shared one family's concern for a lost son.

- A core of people continued to search in spite of discouragement.

- The family's love compelled them to search when all hope was gone.

What a tribute to Joe. True, they did not find him alive. But they loved him and they searched. That search had intrinsic value that defied the outcome.

THINGS VS. PEOPLE

How do you evaluate your personal search efforts?

- With lost objects, success is clear-cut: you either find the object or you don't. Find it and you are successful; fail to find it and you are unsuccessful. Everything fits into tidy categories.

- With lost people, a simplistic assessment is inadequate. There is something inherently significant about a search for a lost person. It communicates love and value. Searching simultaneously becomes a process and an accomplishment. The fact that you search stands as a monument of love and nothing can tear down that monument.

VALUE THE PROCESS

Successful searches do not always have happy endings—that is the truth we find in Lostology Law #22. Joe's tragic story illustrates this law. Other searches affirm the truth.

As lostologists, we value the search process. We celebrate the love, the emotion, the human spirit that compels people to sacrifice and search for lost ones. In a sense, they are successful the moment they begin. No ending can erase the love that prompts the search.

UP FOR EVALUATION

At His death, what did Jesus have to show for three years of intensive searching for the lost? Not much. As He hung naked, nailed to a cross, all but a handful of followers had deserted Him. The crowds that had begged to crown Him king had later cried, "Crucify Him." Objective assessment would have declared His search efforts a failure.

Jesus was the first lostologist to shatter simplistic search evaluations. Jesus' cross demanded that searches be assessed on the basis of total effort—not a one day snapshot and headcount. Jesus' life and death proved that love goes to extraordinary lengths to look for the lost. To focus on who got found was appropriate, but short-sighted. The cross proclaimed that God searched for the lost. The cross declared that love was offered, even if rejected.

No one lost could ever, from that point on, doubt God's love or His willingness to launch a rescue mission. The cross stood as a landmark for lost people throughout time. No matter how many were ultimately found, Jesus' search was successful.

THE SEARCH FOR A NEW CHURCH

We had grand goals when we planned our spiritual search and rescue mission in Portland. At that time, churches were being started in other parts of the country with unprecedented results. Using an innovative telemarketing and direct mail strategy developed by a businessman named

We did this

Norm Whan, new churches were beginning with first Sunday attendance of 300 to 500.[11] Our goal was to go beyond that level.

We set out to contact 80,000 homes. If the statistics held, we would have up to 800 people at our first service. Sustaining an 80,000 dial-up long-distance telemarketing campaign proved too ambitious. In the end, we struggled to reach the 47,000 mark. Still, I told the volunteers to expect between 450 and 500 people at our first service. For that we worked and prayed.

On the first Sunday, of those who received calls and mail from us, around 160 true prospects showed up (209 if we counted everyone who attended, including our volunteers). We never did find the rest of the 47,000 families. A successful search? No way. Or was it?

Our massive search effort did have intrinsic value. Whether people in Portland realized it or not, the fact remained that a spiritual search and rescue operation had been mounted on their behalf. In this project, everyday Christians did a very hard thing: they became "telemarketers for Jesus"—not the culmination of anyone's lifelong dream. Teenagers and adults, young people through grandparents joined the search team. They invested time. The long distance callers invested money. Volunteers addressed mailing labels and prepared bulk mailings. No one could have asked a group to do more than these people did. They searched thoroughly. They searched faithfully. They searched well.

On Sunday night, March 13, 1988, the mother church in Garland, Texas, gathered for their evening service. As arranged, the pastor, Roger McDonald, called me from a phone at the pulpit connected to a speaker so all in the congregation could hear our conversation.

"John," he said, "tell us how it went today." Fearing the people would be disappointed, I paused, then said with a degree of reluctance, "We had 209 in our service this morning."

For the next few moments, I heard nothing but the sound of long-distance applause. The people in the congregation, those dear friends, recognized what I had not understood. Yes, they spontaneously celebrated the results—the people who came. But they also celebrated the search process—the fact that they and others had done a hard thing, a good thing, and reached across America to begin a new church. No one could rob them of their accomplishment. They were true lostologists.

162

New Score Cards

Traditionally, evangelism has focused on results. Unless people pray the prayer and sign the card, we tend to classify the event as unsuccessful. As lostologists, we must expand that narrow concept of evangelism.

As we search for the lost, we will not always find them. Often when we share our faith, our efforts go nowhere. Seekers reject our attempts to tell them about Christ. We return defeated and discouraged.

We must learn to value the search itself. Here are a few marks of success we can celebrate whenever Christians share their faith in any way:

- We can celebrate that Christians took a stand for Christ in a lost world. In a world that lacks conviction and questions if anything is ultimately true, Christians share the good news about the truth that sets people free.

- We can celebrate that Christians stopped talking about how much they believed in evangelism and actually talked to lost people about Jesus. There was a victory of obedience over hypocrisy.

- We can celebrate that Christians demonstrated their love for Christ and for lost people by explaining God's love for them. They refused to stay at church and talk about love. These Christians moved into the world and told lost people that God loved them enough to die for them.

- We can celebrate that Christians confronted lost people with the claims of Christ on their lives. Never again can these non-Christians offer the excuse that they didn't know what God offered to them and demanded from them. Never again can these lost people say that no one cared enough for them to tell them how to be saved.

- We can celebrate that Christians actively participated in Jesus' Great Commission. They went into the world seeking to make disciples. In doing so, they fulfilled their responsibility and prepared to stand before God with the confidence obedience brings.

The fact that we *go*, that we *try*, that we *attempt* to tell others about Christ has intrinsic value. We want to find the lost, but we must never forget the basic principle of lostology: successful searches do not always have happy endings. A search begun is cause for celebration. Every search is a victory.

THE FINAL EVALUATION

Ultimately, God will not hold us accountable for the number of people who respond to our witness. Salvation is an individual responsibility and each person is accountable to God for how they respond to Him.

Yet we as Christians are also accountable to God. When we stand before God, He will look at us and say, "Did you search for My lost ones?"

"Yes, Lord," we will respond. "We searched. We didn't find all we hoped to find. Still we searched."

Then our heavenly Father will say, "Well done, My good and faithful searchers. Well done."

THE LOSTOLOGY LAB

- By what criteria do most Christians and churches evaluate the success of an evangelistic effort? Do you think this criteria is appropriate or adequate? Why or why not?

- When you have talked to lost friends or loved ones about Christ, how did you evaluate your efforts? What criteria did you use for success? Has this portion of your study of lostology changed your criteria? If so, how? If not, why?

- If you had been at Calvary on the day Jesus died on the cross, how would you have assessed the impact of His ministry if all you knew was what you observed that day?

- Imagine that a Christian friend has just returned from church visitation. He talked to a fellow who was not a Christian, but the man was not ready to commit his life to Christ. Your Christian friend is discouraged and feels he has failed in his efforts. Based on your understanding of lostology, how could you encourage your friend to view his evening as a success rather than as a failure?

- If you were to stand before God right now and give an account for the way you have been involved in sharing your faith, what would you say to God? How do you think God would respond to you? Would God affirm that you have been faithful in this area of your Christian life?

Coming Next: Just Be There

Often, the most important part of a search is being there. Good things happen if we are in the right place at the right time. Our next study will help us learn about this dimension of lostology.

When the Lost Find the Searchers

Seek the Lord while He may be found;
call on Him while He is near.
Isaiah 55:6

Lostology Law #23
If you are searching, the lost may find you.

From the first, we feared the worst. Friday evening, the television news reported that three-year-old Joseph Leffler was lost in the woods outside Estacada, Oregon. A massive search was underway.

The lost boy's plight and his parents' anguish captured the hearts of people in the northwest. Throughout the weekend, newspapers and newscasts provided progress reports on the search. Nothing looked promising. How long could a three-year-old survive alone in the densely forested hills? The story continued— Saturday evening, Sunday morning. The dreaded ending appeared inevitable.

Monday morning, July 10, 1988, everything changed. The front page of the *Oregonian* proclaimed the news—Joseph Leffler was safe. Great story. Happy ending. Like a sweet taste, this story lingers years later because of the way the *Oregonian* described the rescue and the headline they ran. Here is an excerpt from that story:

Joseph walked away from home about 1:00 P.M. Friday after telling his mother that he was going fishing. He had taken a three-foot-long section of tube, his favorite pretend fishing pole, to what his parents assumed was the backyard where he usually played.

Joseph was not seen again for nearly 48 hours, prompting a massive search of the area. But, just before noon on Sunday, little Joseph came walking out of the woods and came straight up to one of the searchers.

"I had to look twice," said Judy Magill of Milwaukie, who was coordinating the search dogs. "I couldn't believe this little boy was walking toward me. He stretched out his arms and I picked him up," she said.

Joseph was carried to the command post near the house where his family had been staying. He was placed in a helicopter and flown to the University Hospital in Portland where he was checked and released.[12]

A front page picture showed little Joseph in his mother's arms. He looked bewildered but well. Above the picture in bold block letters the *Oregonian* headline read:

LOST BOY FINDS SEARCHERS

The authors of the story crafted a gem with that headline. Little did they know their headline and Joseph's story would become a case study in lostology.

ENDINGS WE DON'T CONTROL

"Lost Boy Finds Searchers"—that raises some intriguing questions:

- Did Joseph really find the searchers?

- What was the true role of the search team?

- What if no one had been there when Joseph wandered out of the forest?

- What if the person Joseph "found" had hurt rather than rescued him?

Joseph's story had a happy ending. Everything turned out fine and these questions are no longer relevant for him. But Joseph's ordeal raises questions with profound implications for evangelism:

- Are spiritually lost people trying to get found? How we answer this question will determine the motivation level for our search efforts.

- To what degree are we responsible as spiritual searchers to confront people with their lostness and attempt to convince them to get found? Or to what degree is our role more like the searchers in the story: to be in the search area when lost people are ready to be found?

- What if secular people begin to search for spiritual answers and cannot find Christians to help them? Most lost people do not have close Christian friends. Lost people are vulnerable. They cannot discern spiritual truth from error. If we are not where they can find us, will they stumble into religious cults or be enticed by seductive new age philosophies?

Boil it all down and Lostology Law #23 provides this foundational insight: If you are searching, the lost may find you. Simply being there among the lost may be the most important thing we do in evangelism.

Lost People Found Jesus

Jesus was accessible to lost people. He positioned himself among the people. Jesus lived and trained his disciples in the middle of the spiritual search area. He was not cloistered off in a religious retreat or monastery. As He went through life, He watched for lost people who were ready to be found. When they came, Jesus stopped what He was doing and helped them. Over and over again, the lost found the searcher—Jesus.

Duplicating Jesus' Model

Jesus sent His disciples out on search and rescue training missions. With each assignment, He gave them specific instructions about how and where to spend their time. These men were still learning how to search for the lost and how to spot those who were trying to be found. So Jesus gave them clear-cut guidelines:

> When you enter a town and are welcomed, eat what is set before you. Heal the sick who are there and tell them, "The kingdom of God is near you." But when you enter a town and are not welcomed, go into its streets and say, "Even the dust of your town that sticks to our feet we wipe off against you. Yet be sure of this: The kingdom of God is near." (Luke 10:8-10)

In lostology language, Jesus told His disciples to go among the people and search until they bumped into anyone who was trying to get found. They were to search for the lost people who were looking for the searchers.

FUTURE SEARCH TEAMS

At the close of His ministry, Jesus issued the Great Commission to His disciples . . . and to us today:

> All authority in heaven and on earth has been given to me. Therefore go and make disciples of all nations, baptizing them in the name of the Father, and of the Son and of the Holy Spirit, and teaching them to obey everything I have commanded you. And surely I am with you always, to the very end of the age. (Matt. 18:18-20)

Scholars note that Jesus' command to *go* carried the idea "while you are going." The work of discipleship, including evangelism, was to be done as Christians lived among the people. Immediately before His ascension into heaven, Jesus clarified His commission further:

> You will receive power when the Holy Spirit comes on you; and you will be my witnesses in Jerusalem, and in all Judea and Samaria, and to the ends of the earth. (Acts 1:8)

Jesus promised His power for the spiritual search, then He extended the scope of the search. His disciples were challenged to start where they were, in the area closest to where they lived—Jerusalem. Then they were to increase the scope of their concern in progressive concentric circles to the ends of the earth. Jesus knew that lost people would be trying to "get found" throughout the world. His team, disciples then and now, needed to be there searching for those who were seeking God.

READY FOR THOSE WHO WERE READY

In the years since we began our church in Portland, I have reflected on the people who became part of our church as a result of our initial outreach project. I have also reflected on the strategy we used. It was a comprehensive project:

- People received a long-distance phone call inviting them to attend a new church in their area, if they did not already have a church home.

- Over the following weeks, those who responded positively received five brochures telling them about the new church and its future ministry.

- The week before the first service, they received one additional phone call reminding them about the service and encouraging them to attend.

- After the service, people received additional phones calls and letters.

It was a good strategy. People came—not all we had hoped—but many came. The puzzling question is why? Why would anyone come?

- Why would people pass by established churches to attend a new church meeting in a school gymnasium?

- Why would people respond to the invitation of a telemarketer to attend a worship service with people they didn't know?

- Why would people who were bombarded by junk mail every day respond to through-the-mail information about a new church?

The answers are found in God's search activity—not ours. In reality, we did not find the people who showed up at our church. God was already at work in their lives before we called or before we mailed information. We were there beginning a new church as part of God's master plan. God knew people in that area were ready to "get found." He led us to launch a search in that area and those lost people found us.

SAMPLE SEEKERS

Barry and Lynn were like other seekers who found us. Barry had an odd assortment of religious influences from his childhood. But for twenty years, he had not been involved in church and was not interested. Fortunately, his wife, Lynn, got our long-distance phone call and allowed us to send information.

The mail came. They read it. Lynn even posted the reminder card on their refrigerator. On the second week of our church, Barry, Lynn, and their two children walked in and never left. They ultimately became key leaders in our church. I wish we could take credit for finding them. We can't because we didn't. God was at work in their lives. We were searching. They found us.

The Importance of Being There

Searching for seekers is a strange enterprise. We don't know when they will try to "get found." The danger is that once they begin seeking, they may be intercepted by others who will mislead and hurt them. That is why it is imperative that Christians live in search mode, always watching, always searching.

Among the Lost

Here are a few practical things you can do to position yourself among the lost:

- Get to know the people you contact as part of your daily life: your neighbors, your work associates, others. Determine, if possible, if these people are spiritually lost. Initially, you may have difficulty knowing each person's spiritual situation. Make your best assessment based on what you know about the person. If you are in doubt, assume the person is lost. As you go through your daily routine, make it a point to develop your relationships with these people. Look for natural ways to mention your faith and let them know that you are a Christian. As a result, they may come to you when they want to talk about spiritual things.

- Get involved in community activities that will enable you to meet people. School activities, civic organizations, and recreational activities all provide wonderful opportunities to meet people. Develop relationships with them and look for ways to let these new acquaintances know that you are a Christian. Chances are good that some of the people will be seeking spiritual answers and will be glad to know a Christian with whom they can talk.

- Guard against allowing church and fellowship with other Christians to absorb all your time, making it difficult for you to spend any time with non-Christians. This balance requires constant juggling. Obviously, church involvement and Christians fellowship is important. It must not, however, consume all your time and isolate you from the lost people around you.

INCREDIBLE NEEDS

How the world needs Christians who are willing to be accessible to lost people. How we need churches around the world dedicated to helping the lost get found. How we need missionaries to live among the people in countries where there aren't enough churches or perhaps none at all. God is at work around the world drawing lost people to Himself. If we are there, the lost can find us. And if the lost find us, we can make sure the lost find Jesus.

THE LOSTOLOGY LAB

- Refer to the story about Joseph at the beginning of this chapter. Imagine you are Judy Magill, the lady who Joseph "found" when he wandered out of the woods. How would you have felt when you saw the little boy walking up to you and realized he was the lost child? What would you have felt about your search activities up to that point? Would you have felt as if you had found Joseph or as if Joseph had found you? Would it matter?

- How do you view your responsibility in evangelism? Are you supposed to convince people they are lost and lead them to Jesus? Are you supposed to be available to help people find God when they begin to seek Him? Or do you view your responsibility as somewhere between these two extremes?

- Why do you believe so many people today become part of cults and other religions rather than becoming Christians? What principles can you draw from Joseph Leffler's story to help explain your answer?

- How involved are you with lost people? To what degree have you isolated yourself from secular people through your involvement in church activities and Christian fellowship?

- Do the non-Christians you know realize that you are a Christian? How do they know? If any of them wanted to talk with someone about their relationship with God, do you think they would talk with you? Why or why not?

- Jesus spent so much time with lost people that His critics accused Him of being "the friend of sinners." Would anyone accuse you of being the friend of sinners? Would lost people consider you their friend?

COMING NEXT: AFTER THE SEARCH

What is the best way to end a search when the lost are found? What we do and how we respond show the emotions and values we brought to the search all along. We will study the appropriate response in the next chapter.

TWENTY-FOUR

Time to Celebrate

In the same way, I tell you, there is rejoicing
in the presence of the angels of God
over one sinner who repents.
Luke 15:10

Lostology Law #24
Always celebrate when the lost are found.

It was late, too late for such a little girl to be at the airport. But there she was, balloons tied to one arm, a little sign in her hand. Such a little girl walking down the long concourse so late at night. She was wide awake. "Is he here?" she asked those around her. "Is he here?" Knowing nods and smiles. "Not yet, honey," they said. "Not yet."

Tired travelers with carry-on luggage, crumpled suits, and bloodshot eyes glanced at her and smiled. Such a little girl. So late . . . too late.

The little girl walked on, taking two, sometimes three steps for every step the adults took. Still she kept up. "Is he here?" she asked again. "Is he here?"

The entourage led by the tiny balloon bearer arrived at the gate. She stopped. Her balloons bobbed above her head and her sign poked those around her. Fortunately, hers was not a long wait. Unable to contain herself any longer, she began to jump up and down, causing her balloons to bounce and bob and her sign to flop and bend.

Curiosity overcame many strangers that night. They paused and stared. Not knowing why, they looked where the little girl looked. As they watched, the door opened and people streamed up the inclined walkway. One then another they came, men and women, but mostly men, all dressed alike.

And then he came, the one the little girl was waiting for. "Daddy," she squealed as she ran toward one young soldier who dropped to his knees and scooped her in his arms.

As the men and women of Desert Storm flooded the concourse that night, a group of bleary-eyed travelers dropped their carry-on-luggage and crumbled suit coats and began to applaud. But in the midst of the crowd, cradled in her father's arms, one little girl celebrated. Her daddy was home.

SPONTANEOUS CELEBRATION

Celebration is a spontaneous response when we find a lost valuable—a person or a thing. The little girl at the airport did what her heart told her to do that night: she celebrated. Her daddy had been far away . . . lost to her. But he came home. She found him right there in the airport. That night she celebrated.

Celebration is instinctive. No one has to teach us. No one has to say: "At this point, it's important to express a bit of emotion. I suggest you squeal and jump up and down." No one needs instruction. Celebration bubbles up from hearts pressure-packed with joy.

We all celebrate when we find lost valuables. Our response reveals our values. Celebration demonstrates to all who watch that we have reclaimed something of significance, a lost item we treasure or a lost person we love.

Lostologists study the celebration response and have identified Lostology Law #24: Always celebrate when the lost are found. Celebration is so natural that a lack of it indicates something is wrong. In life, celebration occurs regularly. Yet in many churches, Christian respond to the news that someone has become a Christian with polite affirmation rather than heart-felt rejoicing. Such lukewarm response would have been unacceptable to Jesus.

THREE CELEBRATION STORIES

In Jesus' three classic stories about lost valuables, He made celebration the common theme:

- When the shepherd finds the missing sheep, he celebrates: "And when he finds it, he joyfully puts it on his shoulders and goes home. Then he calls his friends and neighbors together and says, 'Rejoice with me; I have found my lost sheep'" (Luke 15:5-6).

- When the woman finds her missing coin, she celebrates: "And when she finds it, she calls her friends and neighbors together and says, 'Rejoice with me; I have found my lost coin'" (Luke 15:9).

- When the father finds his missing son, he celebrates: "But the father said to his servants, 'Quick! Bring the best robe and put it on him. Put a ring on his finger and sandals on his feet. Bring the fattened calf and kill it. Let's have a feast and celebrate. For this son of mine was dead and is alive again; he was lost and is found.' So they began to celebrate" (Luke 15:22-24).

Notice that these were not independent celebrations; these were social events . . . parties. Joy prompted the parties. Parties expressed the celebration. Through the parties and the celebrations, the shepherd, the woman, and the father communicated their deepest values.

- Who could have attended the shepherd's party without sensing the distinctive concern he had for his flock?

- Who could have come to the woman's party without understanding that the coins were treasures to her?

- Who could have come to the father's party without knowing that the father's love embraced the lost son no matter what he had done?

To be sure that no one missed the spiritual implications of these stories, Jesus spelled out the application in clear terms:

"I tell you that in the same way there will be more rejoicing in heaven over one sinner who repents than over ninety-nine righteous persons who do not need to repent" (Luke 15:7).

"In the same way, I tell you, there is rejoicing in the presence of the angels of God over one sinner who repents" (Luke 15:10).

Jesus left no doubt. When the lost are found, celebration occurs in heaven. What happens on earth must mirror the heavenly party in spirit and joy.

177

CELEBRATING NEW LIFE IN CHRIST

My fondest memories of our church in Portland were the times we gathered to celebrate when our seeker friends came to Christ. Our celebration centerpiece was baptism. Baptism was not the solemn church ritual it has become in many established churches. Since we did not have a building, we baptized any place we could find water: community swimming pools, neighborhood pools, and even rivers. These casual settings created the perfect atmosphere for our celebrations.

As our friends moved out into the water signaling the fact they were trusting Christ and had entered into a relationship with him, we all watched with joy. As the person was raised out of the water, our church erupted into applause and cheers.

GATHERING AT THE RIVER

One weekend our church met outside Portland for an all-church campout. On Sunday morning, we worshiped together in an open pavilion on the banks of a beautiful river. After the service, we lined the river bank and watched as numerous adults and children were baptized.

What a sight greeted the fishermen and river-rafters that morning. There we were in the snow-melted ice water, two guys in shirts and swim trunks dunking people under water while a crowd along the bank watched and cheered. Those floating by must have wondered what was going on.

The new Christians who waded into the river never forgot that experience. They gave exuberant reports about the water temperature as they stepped carefully out to deeper water to be baptized. But even soaking wet and freezing cold, they were all smiles and tears as they declared publicly their commitment to follow Christ.

For all of us, new Christians and seasoned veterans, baptism became the perfect way to celebrate a successful search.

VALUES ON DISPLAY

Management consultants Peters and Waterman studied top corporations attempting to understand what enabled these companies to achieve standards of excellence. They wrote about their findings in their books *In Search of Excellence* and *A Passion for Excellence*[13] One factor they identified was core values—the central beliefs that shaped each company. Although embedded in the fabric of these high-performance organizations, their value systems were clearly visible in what the companies celebrated. Carefully planned celebrations revealed and reinforced the values to which these companies were committed.

Churches should celebrate their corporate values, too. Unfortunately, in many churches, when people come to Christ, we miss the opportunity for a full-blown celebration. By doing so, we cast doubt about the priority we claim to place on reaching the lost for Christ. How can we say we value the lost then celebrate so half-heartedly when they are found?

PERSONAL CELEBRATION

You may not be able to influence the way your church responds when lost people become Christians. Traditions and theology may dictate certain behavior. You can, however, celebrate personally. Don't worry; your celebration doesn't have to include high-fives or whoop-whoop cheers. Here are a few suggestions that are a bit more low key, but still significant and joyful:

- Send a personal note to those who become Christians in your church. Express your joy over their decision, and commit yourself to pray for them.

- Discover the people who influenced the new Christians to accept Christ. Call them. Offer to pray with them for their friends.

- Keep track of the spiritual birthdays of those who become Christians in your church. Send them cards on their spiritual birthdays and encourage them to continue to grow.

- Pray regularly for the new Christians in your church. Ask God to protect you from ever taking the miracle of spiritual birth for granted.

There are many appropriate ways to celebrate. Hopefully, your commitment to personal celebration will influence others in your church to join you. To hear that the lost have been found and to greet the news with a yawn is a sure sign of spiritual illness. Celebration can be spontaneous, or it can be intentional. But no matter how, no matter when, we must take time to celebrate.

THE LOSTOLOGY LAB

- Imagine you are meeting with a group of people who come from a culture that doesn't even understand the concept of celebration. You must teach them all they need to know about celebration. How would you begin? How would you explain what celebration means? How would you help them understand when it is appropriate? What would you tell them to do when they are celebrating?

- True celebration is spontaneous. What does spontaneous celebration signify and communicate?

- Recall a time when something happened in your life which prompted you to celebrate spontaneously. What event prompted the celebration? What did you do as part of your celebration?

- In what ways can a celebration reveal your values and priorities?

- If a situation called for celebration, but the people involved didn't celebrate, what could you conclude about them? What questions would you have?

- In your church, how do you respond when people become Christians? Does it include elements of celebration? If so, in what ways?

- What would you conclude about a church in which someone became a Christian but no one celebrated? What would their response tell you about the people and their values?

- Jesus said there is rejoicing in heaven over one sinner who repents. How do you imagine this celebration? How do you picture God? What do you imagine the angels doing?

- You may not be able to influence the celebration your church demonstrates when people become Christians. You can, however, decide to celebrate personally. What can you do to celebrate with those who trust Christ and become Christians?

COMING NEXT: TIME TO SHIFT GEARS

How do you take all you have learned in your study of lostology and use the principles to live in search mode? Get ready for some practical help in the final chapter.

Your Life as a Lostologist

The call to follow Christ is a call to live in *search mode*. To a world lost and disoriented, we must go. It is up to us to find the lost so they can find Jesus Christ. Here are some practical things you can do that will help you live as a lostologist:

Keep Learning About Evangelism Every Time You Get Lost.

- Don't underestimate the fact that some of the non-Christians you meet are having fun . . . at least for the moment. Be patient. Like the seasons, their time of need will come.

- Remember that the non-Christians you meet never intended to get lost spiritually. Never assume they chose to mess up their lives and therefore deserve what has happened to them.

- Never forget how easy it is to be lost spiritually. Remembering this will make you more gracious as you deal with seekers.

- Always remember that most non-Christians are lost and don't know it. Don't assume they recognize their need for God.

- Don't try and force non-Christians to admit they are lost. It's futile.

- Watch for any indication that non-Christians sense they are lost. That awareness is the turning point in their spiritual direction.

Keep Learning How to Give Good Spiritual Directions.

- Your seeker friends hate to feel vulnerable. Be sensitive. Don't push. If you push them, they may get scared and run.

- Don't ever make seekers feel stupid just because they're lost. Don't flaunt your Bible knowledge or spiritual insights. Never "talk down" to seekers. Affirm that they are intelligent people who are just beginning to learn about spiritual things.

- Remember people's reluctance to trust strangers. Give your seeker friends time to trust you. They may find it hard to think about trusting Christ until they decide if they can trust you and what you are telling them about Christ.

- Never underestimate the significance of a spiritual question. Pay attention. When a seeker asks anything, listen. It's important.

- Be patient if your non-christian friends struggle to understand the spiritual directions you are giving. Directions are inherently confusing. Go slow. Keep it simple. Assume your friends know nothing.

- Don't give your seeker friends too much spiritual information. In an attempt to share all you know, you'll confuse rather than help.

Pay the Cost of Searching for the Lost.

- Make time to search for those who are lost spiritually. Participating in the search is the only way to show that you really value lost people. Anything else is just cheap talk.

- Be prepared to pay the price in time and money to reach lost people. Spiritual search and rescue are inherently costly. Don't expect any discounts.

- A spiritual search always begins with your heart and the love you feel for spiritually lost people. If you don't love the lost, ask God to change your heart.

- Make time in your schedule for reaching out to non-Christians. Don't allow other priorities to crowd this top priority off your list.

- Take the initiative to go to spiritually lost people and adapt to them. Don't expect them to come and adapt to you. Be willing to enter their world and tell them about Christ, rather than bringing them into your world before you talk with them about Christ.

- Let the reality of hell create an appropriate sense of urgency in your heart as you seek to share Christ with lost people. They are in danger of spending eternity without God. Your search is a race against time.

Master the Secrets of a Successful Search.

- Work to gain additional skills in reaching non-Christians and telling them about Christ. Use what you learn to help other Christians get involved along with you. Working with others will multiply your effectiveness.

- Learn to pace yourself in your spiritual life so you are less vulnerable to discouragement. Remember that you can accomplish incredible things if you do not give up.

- Recognize when you've shifted into the "waiting phase" in your attempts to reach certain people. Use the waiting times to increase your prayer life and to build your faith. Always expect the lost to come home.

- Discipline yourself to call every search a success no matter what happens. Thank God that He will count you faithful because you search for the lost, not just when you find the lost.

- Never stop seeking the lost. Sometimes, while you're looking for the lost, spiritual seekers will find you.

- Always celebrate when the lost are found. Involve others in your celebration. Lead your church to make these celebrations a high point in your community of faith.

Were you counting? That was twenty-four ways you can understand and help spiritually lost people. Follow these guidelines and you will be a lostologist. (And you won't be obnoxious!) A world of spiritually lost people is waiting for you. Now you are ready to find them.

The 24 Laws of Lostology

1. Being lost can be fun.

2. No one gets lost on purpose.

3. It is easy to get lost.

4. You can be lost and not know it.

5. You cannot force people to admit they are lost.

6. Admitting you are lost is the first step in the right direction.

7. When you are lost, you are out of control.

8. Just because you are lost does not mean you are stupid.

9. It is tough to trust a stranger.

10. People ask for directions without revealing their true emotions.

11. Directions are always confusing.

12. Unnecessary details make directions more confusing.

13. A search reveals your values.

14. Searches are always costly.

15. Love pays whatever a search costs.

16. A search becomes your consuming priority.

17. A search is always lost-centered, not searcher-centered.

18. A search is urgent because the lost are in danger.

19. Coordinate resources to maximize the search.

20. Discouragement threatens a successful search.

21. Waiting is part of searching.

22. Successful searches do not always have happy endings.

23. If you are searching, the lost may find you.

24. Always celebrate when the lost are found.

Notes

1. Woodstock: Three Days of Peace and Music, *The Director's Cut.* Warner Brothers, Inc. (©1970, 1994) a film directed by Michael Wadleigh, produced by Bob Maurice.

Chapter 1

1. Lloyd Cory, *Quotable Quotations* (Wheaton, Illinois: Victor Books, 1985), 354.

2. For additional information see Ken Hemphill, *Life Answers: Making Sense of Your World* (Nashville, Tennessee: Lifeway Press, 1992). For more information call 1-800-458-2772.

Chapter 7

3. Faith Popcorn, *The Popcorn Report* (New York, New York: Doubleday Currency, 1991), 27-28.

Chapter 12

4. For information about the Continuing Witnessing Training course, write Home Mission Board, SBC, 1350 Spring St., NW, Atlanta, GA, 30367-5601 or call 1-800-634-2462.

5. James Kennedy, *Evangelism Explosion*, (Wheaton, Illinois:Tyndale House Publishers, 1970).For more information about this training course, call 1-305-491-6100.

Chapter 16

6. *Bridge To Life*, (NavPress, 1969). For more information, write The Navigators, P.O. Box 35001, Colorado Springs, CO 80935.

7. *How to Have a Full and Meaningful Life* (The Sunday School Board of the Southern Baptist Convention, 1971). To order a copy, call 1-800-458-BSSB.

8. Bill Bright, *The Four Spiritual Laws* (Campus Crusade For Christ, 1965). For more information write Campus Crusade for Christ International, Arrowhead Springs, San Bernardino, CA 92414.

Chapter 17

9. Frank Voight, *The Lifesaving Station* (Note: unable to verify the author of this work or locate the publication from which this story was taken)

Chapter 19

10. Robert Coleman, *The Master Plan of Evangelism* (Old Tappan, New Jersey: Power Books, 1977), 33.

Chapter 22

11. For more information about *The Phone's for You* by Norm Whan, write Church Growth Development International,420 W. Lambert, Suite E., Brea, CA 92621 or call 1-714-990-9551.

Chapter 23

12. Janet Goetze, Steven Amick, and John Snell, "Lost Boy Finds Searchers," *The Oregonian*, July 10, 1989.

13. Thomas Peters and Robert Waterman, Jr., *In Search of Excellence* (New York, New York: Warner Books, 1982) and Tom Peters and Nancy Austin, *A Passion for Excellence* (New York, New York, 1985).